# God Moments
Direction downloads for living
## Kate Case

## About the Author

Kate lives in Brisbane with her husband, Tony. She graduated in 1980 as a veterinarian but currently works with her husband in their financial planning practice in Brisbane. You can access more information about Tony and Kate, and TC Ministries, from the TC Ministries website at www.tcministries.com.au.

**Dedication**

For Tony, my soul mate. I feel wonderful when I put my hand in his, and he feels gorgeous when he puts his hand in mine!

# God Moments by Kate Case

Copyright © 2013 by Kate Case. All rights reserved.

This book or parts thereof may not be reproduced in any form, stored in a retrieval system, or transmitted in any form by any means - electronic, mechanical, photocopy, recording or otherwise - without prior written permission of the author or publisher, except as provided by Australian copyright law.

Scripture quotations marked "NKJV" are taken from the New King James Version®. Copyright © 1982 by Thomas Nelson, Inc. Used by permission. All rights reserved.

Scripture quotations marked (NIV) are taken from the Holy Bible, New International Version®, NIV®. Copyright © 1973, 1978, 1984 by Biblica, Inc.TM Used by permission of Zondervan. All rights reserved worldwide. www.zondervan.com

This is a publication of TC Ministries
C/- 30/120 Bloomfield Street
Cleveland QLD Australia 4163
admin@tcministries.com.au

ISBN: 978 0 9808793 0 8

## Acknowledgements

I would like to thank everyone who took their time to read my various draft manuscripts and pass onto me their feedback. I have found that feedback, together with the delete key, to be the most valuable tools that a writer can use to shape their work. In addition, I have also found that feedback can provide a focal point for further creative inspiration.

A huge thank you goes to Mark Case for his amazing cover design and graphic layout of the text.

Lastly, I would like to thank my husband, Tony, for being there and being my greatest fan.

# Contents

God Moments (poem)   3
Introduction   4

**Chapter 1: When you least expect them**   6
Mobile Moment   7
Incense Burners   8
The Birthday Present   10

**Chapter 2: Digging in the garden**   12
The Constant Gardener   13
The Discipline of Pruning   14
Going Nutty with Nutgrass   17
The Empty Nest   18
Hanging onto Dead Things   19
Eradicating Locusts   21

**Chapter 3: Watching a film**   26
Facing the Enemy   27
Trophies on the Billiard Room Wall   29
The Gran Torino   30
Looking Ghost Rider in the Eye   32
The Mines of Moria   34

**Chapter 4: Playing a game**   36
Confronting Diablo   37
Superheroes   38
Band-Aids for a Broken Heart   41

**Chapter 5: Anytime, anywhere**   44
A Breakfast Bowl Moment   45
A Shopping Trolley Moment   47
When the Sparks Fly   49
Morning Walk (poem)   51

## Chapter 6: On your knees in prayer     52
A Father's Heart     53
Falling Leaves (poem)     55

## Chapter 7: In the post     58
Fridge Door Art     59
Christmas Card Contemplation     60
Tiny Hands (poem)     62

## Chapter 8: Cooking up a storm     64
Beans on Toast     65
Guess Who's Coming to Dinner     66
A Little Faith Cooking     68

## Chapter 9: Forlorn in sheer frustration     72
Through the Looking Glass     73
Unlocking God's Blessing     74
A Miracle Moment     76

## Chapter 10: Crying out in desperation     78
God's Wrecking Ball     79
The Guilt Trap     80
Light Up Your Life     83
Feathers (poem)     87
Unplugged     89

## Chapter 11: Sharing time with friends     94
The Yoke of Freedom     95
The School Reunion     96
Gift Wrapped     98
No Time to Say Goodbye     99

## Chapter 12: Any old how     102
Taking the Journey     103
Balthazar (poem)     107

## **God Moments**

You can have them
    When least expected
You can get them
    Digging in the garden
You can have them
    Watching a film
You can get them
    Playing a game
You can have them
    Any time, anywhere
You can get them
    On your knees in prayer
You can receive them
    In the post
You can get them
    Cooking up a storm
You can have them
    Forlorn in sheer frustration
You can get them
    Crying out in desperation
You can have them
    Sharing time with friends
You can get them
    Any old how
In fact
    I think I'm getting one now...

Kate Case 2011

# Introduction

I love looking out of my kitchen window into my lovely garden. It is with great satisfaction, I think of the hours that I have spent there, replacing the garden soil, carefully nurturing the plants, pruning, watering and fertilising. There are some potted shrubs around our pool that are a constant mass of blooms and are always magnificent to gaze upon from a distance. However, on one occasion, on closer inspection I discovered that in spite of all their magnificence they were riddled with mildew and scale.

This was an ideal opportunity for God to remind me that sometimes not all is at it seems. Just because the grass looks greener on the other side of the fence, doesn't necessarily mean it's more palatable. All that glitters is not gold. We often judge by external appearances but it is God who judges by what he discerns in a man's heart.

Over the years, I have found God to be a Person of surprisingly few words. What I mean is; I don't often hear Him speak out loud to me. On the occasions when He has, it's been with just a few authoritative words such as "Not Yet" or "Stand Firm".

On the other hand, I have found Him to be a Person of great moments. Times, when through the little things in life, He has revealed to me some of the great truths about the world in which we live and the endless Love that He has for each of us. Through these moments I have learnt that God is always talking to us; that He is in endless dialogue with us. You may tend to think that God is silent most of the time, especially if you are expecting Him to communicate with you audibly through spoken words.

Do not be mistaken. He is not silent. Every moment of your life is an opportunity for communication with God.

Over the years I have had some truly inspirational moments with God, often when I least expected them. He never ceases to surprise with what He often has to say or how He uses seemingly insignificant events to reveal some profound truths. God meets us where we are.

You too can hear from God, if you learn to be still and listen for His voice in your circumstances.

This book is meant to be savoured as you would your favourite meal - one mouthful at a time. So don't rush through it - take your time. Enjoy and may you too find God in the simple things of life.

"For in Him we live and move and have our being"
Acts 17:28 (NKJV)

## Chapter One:
**God moments can happen when you least expect them...**

# A Mobile Moment

On one occasion at work I had been trying to make contact with a client who wanted to come in to see my husband for some advice. I never seemed to be able to reach her by phone in order to actually settle on a time. One morning, I picked up her file and just put it on my desk as a follow up job for the day. Later that morning, I felt prompted to give her a call right there and then. So, I did.

To my surprise, the lady who answered the phone was not our client but an employee of a supermarket chain in a town many miles away from where our client lived. She said, "We were wondering whose phone this was!"

It turned out that our client had dropped her phone in the supermarket car park that morning. Later I learned that at the time she did not even know that she had lost it. I alerted my client's workplace and the phone was eventually retrieved. The next day our client called and made an appointment!

God truly works in mysterious ways.

"For as the heavens are higher than the earth, so are
My ways higher than your ways, and My thoughts
than your thoughts."
Isa 55:9 (NKJV)

Never underestimate God and His ability to intervene with power in your life in order to mesh your desires into His ultimate and perfect purposes.

What happened to me that day was one of those "Wow" moments that you get sometimes with God. It gave me a new perspective on God and my role in His kingdom. It helped me appreciate just how much God loves to use us to bring blessing unexpectedly into other people's lives.

God has the big picture and we don't always get to see God's perspective until we step out in faith in response to His call to action. Two people got blessed that day; our client and me. Neither of us was expecting it to happen and neither of us actually asked for it!

God didn't tell me verbally to call our client. It was one of those moments that you just know is a "God Prompt"; A deep inner forceful conviction that urges you to do something now. Confirmation that it was from God came after and not before I responded to it.

I could have ignored the inner prompting. Just let it pass by. God is not pushy. I could have passed up another great moment with God.

It's those unexpected expressions of love and kindness that invigorate relationships and strengthen the bonds of friendship. We walk in a love relationship with God and I think at times He just likes to surprise us with moments that re-enforce His love towards us. They are a reminder that God is always there, always caring for us.

"The LORD himself goes before you and will be with
you; he will never leave you nor forsake you.
Do not be afraid; do not be discouraged."
Deut 31:8 (NIV)

# Incense Burner

I couldn't sleep one night, so I got up. It seemed pointless to just lie there staring at the ceiling in a dreamless gloom punctuated with snuffling snores. As I got to the top of the stairs, I sensed a wonderful aroma filling the house. The cleaners had been the day before, so I thought it must have been due to some new product they had been using.

As I got to the bottom of the stairs, there was a glow emanating from the family room. My initial thought was; "We are lucky the house hasn't burnt down!" My husband had forgotten to extinguish the candles before coming to bed some hours ago. Maybe this was why God had disturbed my sleep?

But no! I then thought about the temple of God in the Old

Testament. The burning of incense was one of the most highly sought after responsibilities in the temple. A sacrifice of incense was burned twice daily; in the morning when the lamps were dressed and in the evening when the lamps were lit. The penalty of death hung over anyone who profaned their duties.

The temple was constantly filled, twenty-four hours a day, with the most wonderful aromas. It stuck me that God not only wanted His place to look good, He also wanted it to smell good too. Who would ever have thought God was into aromatherapy!

Think about the woman who came to Jesus with an alabaster jar of very expensive perfume made of pure nard (Mk 14:6). She broke open the jar and poured the perfume on His head. This potent fragrance would have permeated every corner of the room and everyone in it. Jesus response was not to rebuke her but to commend her for her sacrifice because "she had done a beautiful thing" (NIV).

It is a well known fact that an aroma can greatly influence a person's wellbeing. Anyone who has had to change a baby's nappy or stood in a crowded lift next to a sweaty body can attest to that!

When you think about it, we live not just in a 'feel-good' and 'look-good' society but also in a 'smell-good' one as well. Think of all the products advertised daily just to make our surroundings and ourselves smell pleasant and attractive to others. You can walk into any candle shop and buy candles with scents that are meant to provoke all types of moods and memories.

Jesus was an incense burner:

"Be imitators of God, therefore, as dearly loved children and
live a life of love, just as Christ loved us and gave himself up
for us as a fragrant offering and sacrifice to God"
Eph 5:1-2 (NIV)

Incense was burnt to make God's Dwelling Place a pleasant place to be. Entering into and lingering in God's Presence was meant to be a calming and soothing experience. We are God's modern day temple and like Jesus, are called to be incense burners, in order to attract others into the Presence of God.

And what is the incense we burn? – A life of love!

# The Birthday Present

Birthdays are really special times and that hasn't diminished as I have gotten older. The only thing I have noticed as you get older is that the birthday party guests tend to go home earlier. All those at my 50th had left and were tucked up in bed by 11pm!

My husband always makes a big effort to make my birthdays a memorable occasion and my 50th birthday was no exception.

He took me as a big surprise into a jewellery shop and said that I could have anything that I liked. Anything. No matter what the cost. Whatever was my heart's desire, I could have. No strings attached.

A hard choice to make with so much to choose from. As I was perusing all the glittering gems, I felt myself saying: Could this really be true? Can I really have my heart's desire? Does the cost really not matter? Do I really deserve this? Am I really that special?

There was no catch. I did not have to promise or do anything for him. My wonderful husband was true to his word and did exactly what he had promised. He bought all the items I had selected; some beautiful deep blue sapphire earrings with a matching ring and pendant.

As I left the store overwhelmed with gratitude and in awe of my husband's love for me, I thought: Nobody has ever done anything like this for me before - ever.

Then I thought: No I am wrong. There is someone. His name is Jesus. He said to me:

"It is done. I am the Alpha and the Omega, the Beginning and the End. To him who is thirsty I will give to drink without cost

from the spring of the water of life."
Rev 21:6 (NIV)

"But God demonstrates his own love for us in this:
While we were still sinners, Christ died for us."
Rom 5:8 (NIV)

"For it is by grace you have been saved, through faith -
and this not from yourselves, it is the gift of God -
not by works, so that no one can boast."
Eph 2:8-9 (NIV)

Jesus had also given me a birthday present many years ago. A born again birthday present. It was then that I realised how much I sometimes take for granted that great free gift of life that God had given to me.

He deserves nothing less than my eternal appreciation for what it cost Him to give it.

God's love for us is a no strings attached love and yes; we are that special to Him. So special, that there was no cost too great to pay in order to secure for us His gift of eternal life. My husband's bank account suffered a bit of a setback for his gift to me, but for Jesus, paying the price for his gift of life meant a vile and hideously painful death.

Jesus' gift to me was far more precious and costly than sapphires.

He gave me His all. He gave me His life.

Everyday - not just on Birthdays.

## Chapter Two:
**God moments can happen digging in the garden...**

# The Constant Gardener

My husband asked me recently when my garden would be completed. Well, gardening is like cleaning and that's why I think God created Adam and Eve to look after His garden. He knew it would take an eternity to finish!

A garden is a living creation requiring constant care; weeding, pruning, planting and watering. It is constantly evolving, constantly changing. If you've ever looked after one you'll know what I mean. One of the very first things that I learnt about my garden is that no plant is forever.

All plants have a life span which determines their time of usefulness within the garden. Some bloom and thrive just for a season while others may last a couple of years before they become too woody and no longer productive. They then need to be removed, in order to make way for fresh life.

Just as portrayed in that wonderful children's movie, "The Lion King", there is indeed a circle of life in the garden. It's a humbling thought and it brings to mind some verses from Psalm 103:

"For he knows how we are formed, he remembers that we are dust. As for man, his days are like grass, he flourishes like a flower of the field; the wind blows over it and it is gone, and its place remembers it no more. But from everlasting to everlasting the Lord's love is with those who fear him and his righteousness..."
Psa 103:14 -17 (NIV)

We may be dust but it does not necessarily mean that we are worthless, like floor sweepings that are gathered up at the end of the day and thrown away. Remember, this is the dust that God breathed His own Spirit of Life into in the Garden of Eden. It is also this dust that Jesus gave His life blood for on a cross.

On the other hand, if you read about what happened in the Garden of Eden (Genesis 3) you will see that was also the dust that rebelled and thought itself an equal to God. It thought itself wise enough to judge God and His intentions!

For that reason, more often than not, we do well to remember that we are dust. Sometimes we presume too much of God and like Job, similarly deserve God's rebuke to him from out of the storm:

"Where were you when I laid the earth's foundation? Tell me, if you understand. Who marked off its dimensions? Surely you know!
Who stretched a measuring line across it? On what were its footings set, or who laid its cornerstone while the morning stars sang together and all the angels shouted for joy?"
Job 38:4-7 (NIV)

So what kind of dust are we then? In spite of what happened we are not worthless but precious dust. A dust that contains millions of precious seeds, planted there by God.

We need to find contentment in that unique place that God has placed us. We need to blossom and grow where we have been planted, for however long that season is on this earth. It is not our place to tell the Gardener where to plant us but it is our responsibility to make the most of all the nutrients that we have been given to promote growth.

When it's all done and dusted we will walk into eternity as a friend of the Gardener who planted us there.

"Blessed is the man who walks not in the counsel of the ungodly,
nor stands in the path of sinners, nor sits in the seat of the scornful;
But his delight is in the law of the LORD, and in His law he meditates
day and night. He shall be like a tree planted by the rivers of water,
That brings forth its fruit in its season, whose leaf also shall
not wither; and whatever he does shall prosper."
Psa 1:1-3 (NKJV)

# The Discipline of Pruning

I have a number of shrubs in my garden which require constant attention with regards to pruning. In particular, there is a bottlebrush in the middle of a garden bed outside our front door. If left to their own devices, these types of plants, over the years, grow tall and woody. In fact they can become rather unsightly if they are not regularly pruned back into shape. Pruning takes time and it can seem almost cruel to the plant to be cutting off so much vegetation. Yet, it never ceases to amaze me how resilient plants can be; responding to the harsh cut of the knife with so much vigorous verdant growth, soon to be followed by an abundance of blossoms.

We are no different to the shrubs in my garden, as John reminds us in his Gospel.

"I am the true vine, and My Father is the vinedresser.
Every branch in Me that does not bear fruit, He takes away;
and every branch that bears fruit, He prunes it,
that it may bear more fruit."
Jn 15:1-2 (NKJV)

The harsh times in our lives, that things that hit us out of left field, can retrospectively be seen as blessings in disguise. They are pruning experiences; times for cutting away what it is not important and non-productive; for refocusing on and taking stock of the essential in our lives.

Interestingly it also says in the verses below that it is the productive branches, not the non-productive one, that get pruned. It is the non-fruit bearing branches that are taken away and burned! Pruning might be painful at the time, but submitting to it can produce a multitude of blessings and enhance your usefulness to the Kingdom of God.

If we tend to think of God our Father purely as a God of love who is going to give us an endlessly happy and pain free existence, we will soon become disillusioned. Every time something goes wrong and hurts us we will end up blaming God for not protecting us. Such a concept of God is not endorsed by Scripture nor does it mesh with reality.

"He who spares his rod hates his son, But he who loves him
disciplines him promptly."
Prv 13:24 (NKJV)

This is not to say that the evil and harm that comes into our lives is orchestrated by God. But the resurrection power of our Heavenly Father is such, that anything that comes into our lives, good or bad, if submitted to his pruning knife will ultimately only produce blessing in our lives.

If we are honest with ourselves, much of the harm that does come into our lives is self inflicted or self induced. Those are the times that we choose to go our own way, ignore good counsel and make foolish decisions. We end up becoming like twisted and warped branches on the vine, in need of God's pruning to bring productivity back into our lives. Feeling the consequences for our actions is a good pruning tool. If God were to continually shield us from the pain of our foolish decisions it would not be love. By never facing the consequences' of our actions, we grow wild and wayward - rebellious and unproductive. Remember, these are the type of branches that are eventually removed and burned.

Times of testing will come into our lives even during the periods of blessing when things actually seem to be going well. It is in these times of adversity that the Holy Spirit will bring to maturity within our character the fruits of love, peace, patience, compassion and joy.

So welcome the pruning knife with joy. It makes way for a bountiful harvest.

"But the fruit of the Spirit is love, joy, peace, patience,
kindness, goodness, faithfulness, gentleness and self-control.

Against such things there is no law."
Gal 5:22-23 (NIV)

Loving discipline by our Heavenly Father turns us into effective disciples.

# Going Nutty with Nutgrass

Without a doubt, nutgrass would have to be one of the most resilient and frustrating weeds that I have had to eradicate from my garden. If you are a gardener you will have some sympathy for my viewpoint. I have tried all sorts of chemical eradication techniques without great success as it is a very persistent weed. The only effective solution I have arrived at is to immediately remove any that I find with a spade. Why do I hate this weed? Well, this is one of the few weeds which I know of, that can actually lead to destruction of an entire garden bed if left unchecked.

On the surface of the soil it might look like a few green shoots, but underneath there lurks an intricate webbed root system that links all the nut grass plants together. It is this root system, along with underground nuts, that must be removed in order to prevent re-infestation. If the weeds are ignored, this root system will undermine and interlace with every plant in the garden. The ultimate final solution is to dig up the entire garden bed, removing and discarding all plants and soil and then to completely start over with fresh soil and plants.

How often have you ignored things that bothered or irritated you, only to find later, that they haven't gone away, but in fact have gotten worse? Unresolved hurts, anger and conflict can give rise to the roots of bitterness which can totally undermine our personal peace and cause relational disharmony.

Bitterness and resentment can be very insidious. They tend to slowly creep into our lives, almost unnoticed and can end up gaining a stranglehold on hearts and emotions. What can start out as legitimate anger can then easily be transformed into a desire to seek revenge and inflict hurt on others for the wrongs they have caused us. So begins the breakdown of relationships and sometimes estrangement of once good friends. It is especially sad when this occurs within the fellowship of believers - amongst people who should know better!

If you find yourself overreacting to what might seem a minor wrong, welling up with an anger that is not easily pacified, then perhaps there is a root of bitterness taking hold. Usually this is given permission to grow due to some past unresolved hurt or wrong; something that we have chosen to ignore because it's too hard or too painful to deal with.

The only way to root out bitterness is with forgiveness - by the spadeful. We need to be vigilant spade wielders against all the weeds of bitterness - otherwise we'll go nuts!

"Pursue peace with all people, and holiness, without which
no one will see the Lord: looking carefully lest anyone fall short
of the grace of God; lest any root of bitterness springing up
cause trouble, and by this many become defiled."
Heb 12:14-15 (NKJV)

# The Empty Nest

As a result of living in a coastal environment, we occasionally experience strong overnight winds. One morning I found a partly constructed bird's nest lying on our patio tiles. Each morning during the previous week when I looked out my kitchen window I had seen one of the doves that live in our garden come down and pick up a piece of shredded palm leaf in its beak. Now I could see for myself what they had been constructing. I wondered what conversation the birds might have had that morning as they looked down upon their creation lying in ruins on my garden patio?

Do you think it might have gone like this?

"OOooo... Do you think it's a sign from God? Do you think God wants us to build a nest this year? Do you think we should adopt and give up on eggs? COOoooo"

Well of course, in reality the birds would just get on with building another nest, because it's that time of year when they are motivated instinctively to do so.

Life can often throw curved balls at us and frustrate our plans. It's even more frustrating when we believe we have been walking in God's blessing and according to His will for our lives. When disaster strikes we begin to inwardly doubt and question our purposes and plans.

Consider this. If the winds had not come until after the doves had completed their nest and it was occupied by nestlings, wouldn't that have been a greater disaster; only then to find out that there had been a construction fault in the nest?

Sometimes our plans need frustrating. It can be a positive and not a negative thing. It does not mean that our intentions or directions are wrong - maybe just the way we were going about it.

"Consider it all joy, my brethren, when you encounter various trials, knowing that the testing of your faith produces endurance. And let endurance have its perfect result, that you may be perfect and complete, lacking in nothing."
Jas 1:2-4 (NIV)

# Hanging onto Dead Things

There are a number of palm trees that line our back fence on our neighbour's side. If you have palm trees in your garden you will appreciate that while they might add to the tropical ambience of a garden, they produce a lot of mess in the process. I am constantly sweeping and picking up palm frond fragments, nuts and branches. We have a swimming pool at that side of the fence, so there is also added work in keeping the pool free of mess as well.

I looked out one day and noticed that one of these palms had a very large frond hanging vertically alongside its trunk by what seemed to be small sinewy attachment at its base. That frond hung there for many days. I thought surely with the wind that comes it would loosen and drop to the ground below. It was very unsightly, so I decided to try to remove it myself.

An easy task I thought! One yank and it would come loose and fall. Not so! It took a considerable amount of force and much yanking to finally dislodge it.

This frond was no longer of any use to the tree. It had no life in it but the palm tree still seemed reluctant to give it up. It reminded me of a child with a loose baby tooth, not wanting its parent to give it the final yank to remove it.

Too painful a thought! Better to just have it wobbling or dangling there, they think! Too hard to let go!

I smiled inwardly. There were plenty of times in my life when, like the palm, I had hung onto dead things.

Unfortunately my first marriage was one of those dead things. That it had died was obvious to my closest friends but I was not willing to let go of it. My fervent belief was that a Christian marriage should never end in divorce. Yes, I had read those books that urge Christian wives to hold onto the hope that God would one day, against all odds, reconcile them to their estranged husbands. Perhaps good advice for some and perhaps even good advice for you, but not appropriate for me.

I did not want to let go of my old life even though the life had gone from it. God had to prise my fingers loose from it and when I finally accepted His permission to let go, such a heavy weight lifted from my heart.

Clinging to the dead things of life can cause great emotional and spiritual trauma and can even lead to physical illness, as was the case with me. Now dead things are not just relationships but could be fervently held beliefs or ideas, dreams, hobbies, possessions, pleasures and even old hurts; things that no longer have any life giving value to us but which we still choose to cling to ever so firmly.

In spite of what happened to me, I still believe that God is in the business of relational restoration and that it does pain Him greatly when our human relationships fail. I am not advocating divorce, but when a marriage fails there are no innocent parties. Both people are accountable before God for their actions and choices. I only know that for me, in my situation, the only way forward was to let go of my old life.

Letting go does not mean giving up, nor does it mean that all hope is lost. It does however allow for new growth to take place. Before adult teeth can grow, baby teeth must fall out; old leaves must wither and be shed before new shoots can emerge.

I felt no condemnation from God in letting go – only peace. One month after I did this, I met for the first time the wonderful man who is now my soul mate. God did not restore me to my first husband but he did restore me and my faith in marriage. Who knows, maybe one day there will also be a form of restoration for those broken relationships from my old life as well.

"Then He who sat on the throne said, Behold, I make all things new." Rev 21:5 (NKJV)

There is a very good reason why we need to let go of dead things. The things of value that die in our lives have often withered because of some underlying sinful behaviour or pattern that is rooted deep within ourselves. Failing to let go is a refusal to acknowledge this and impedes the restorative and reviving work of the Holy Spirit.

The day I let go, I let God begin a restoration work in me.

# Eradicating Locusts

I love roses but they can be the most finicky plants to grow in a coastal sub-tropical environment. They seem to readily succumb to any one of a myriad of problems. I have a whole shelf in my garden shed devoted to rose care. Sprays for all sorts of pests ranging from scale to white mites, red mites, caterpillars, fungal growths and rots, black spot and grasshoppers. You name it, roses seem to get it! If not treated at the first sign of infestation, it can quickly become a terminal disaster for the plant.

The effort is worth it, especially when the plants burst into a mass of fragrant blooms. One morning I discovered a caterpillar munching its way into the concealed and enfolded petals of a rose bud. All that focused growth and magnificence, destroyed in a few caterpillar munching moments. Urgh!

Grasshoppers are the absolute worst as they can rapidly decimate a whole plant in hours. A few years ago we drove through a locust plague in country Victoria. The air was thick with them and you daren't get out of the car for fear of inhaling them. Every plant in their path was stripped bare and a barren wasteland was left in their wake. Absolutely devastating for farmers already struggling after years of drought.

I used to teach part-time at TAFE (a tertiary technical college). At the beginning of each year I would talk to my students about the four D's: Death, Disease, Disaster and Divorce. If any one of these life events in their own lives directly impacted their ability to hand in work on time and they could prove it, it would be deemed an acceptable excuse. Without fail, every year a few of the students would encounter at least one of the four Ds. One year I did actually have a student encounter a fifth D: the "Dog ate my assignment" "D" - she showed me the teeth marks!

All of us I am sure have times in our lives that have been ravaged and desolated by at least one of the four D's. Times that have been full of apparent wasted time, regret, pain and frustrated hopes. Their effects can be far reaching, leaving life long scarring for some. Just like what the caterpillars did to my rose buds. These buds might eventually open but the blooms are always deformed.

My home life as a teenager was not a happy one and I know at times I used to envy those friends who seemed to have such a normal loving family. My father became very ill when I was eight years old and ceased working. As a consequence, we lived on the poverty line, not being able to afford the nice clothes my friends had or any of the other basic essentials that most people take for granted.

My father suffered not only physically but also mentally. He became so self-absorbed that he was totally incapable of giving his daughters the emotional nurturing and support necessary to grow them into womanhood. Those years were an emotional desert for me, full of thorns and prickles, and I emerged from them emotionally stunted and vulnerable.

When my marriage of twenty years fell apart, I found myself alone and depressed. Yet it was during this time that God chose:

"to restore to me the years the locusts have eaten"
Joe 2:25 (NIV)

He gave me back my teenage years. Being on my own was actually a blessing. No one else to think about other than myself for a change. No husband. No family. No children.

God actually wound back the clock, not physically of course but emotionally. I found inside me that wildness and carefreeness that had eluded me as a young girl but which teenagers seem to thrive on. I felt myself starting to grow up on the inside; growing emotionally into the woman God had always intended me to be.

For the first time in my life I developed an interest in clothes and my outward appearance and even started to discover my own fashion style. I came to appreciate myself as a woman of beauty, like a magnificent red rose without defect in bloom.

This was the "magic" of the Holy Spirit worked on a deformed rosebud. True to His word God restored to me what the locusts had eaten.

So don't loose hope. God is in the restoration business:

"Behold, I make all things new."
Rev 21:5 (NKJV)

Restoration can be a time consuming process, so be patient. Anyone who has lovingly restored an antique piece of furniture will know it is a process that cannot be hurried.

At the heart of all dysfunction in our lives is a spiritual dysfunction. So, the process of restoration usually begins here, with spiritual healing, and then overflows into emotional and physical renewal as well.

The flowers will bloom again in the desert. Where there is barrenness, God offers the promise of life.

"And the desert shall rejoice and blossom as the rose; It shall blossom abundantly and rejoice, even with joy and singing... They shall see the glory of the Lord, the excellency of our God."
Isa 35:1-2 (NKJV)

God Moments

## Chapter Three:
## God moments can happen
# watching a film...

## **Facing the Enemy**

It is just on dawn and the early morning mist is rising through the pine forest. But this is not just the beginning of another day, this is to be the day of great battle where the military might of Rome will face the ferocity of the Germanic Hun. General Maximus exhorts his troops and commanders to face the enemy with courage and the expectation of victorious glory. This man does not show fear, but exudes an aura of steadfast confidence in the face of what he knows will be another gruelling day on the battlefield.

I'm sure you must be familiar with film "Gladiator." Even though Maximus is victorious in battle; he is eventually betrayed and left for dead. The irony for him is that he finally comes back to Rome not as a victorious General but as a Gladiator. Clad in his gladiatorial garb, he stands looking through bars into the arena. In those last few moments before the gate is raised on his adversary, he is not trembling in fear, but stands firm, exhorting His fellow combatants to do the same and to work together. This is a man who carries victory in his heart.

Maximus knew that it was not the Germanic Hun or even his Gladiatorial adversary waiting for him in the arenas that were his real enemies. It was fear. It is no different for us as Christians. Jesus continually exhorted his followers not to be afraid – "To fear not". Whatever it is we fear in our lives, that circumstance, that person, that disease, whatever it is, that thing that we fear will eventually gain victory in our lives because we are afraid of it.

The night before His execution Jesus encouraged His disciples:

"These things I have spoken to you, that in Me you may have peace. In the world you have tribulation, but take courage I have overcome the world."
Jn 16:33 (NKJV)

Just like Maximus we need to face each day with victory in our hearts.

"For whatever is born of God overcomes the world; and this is the victory that has overcome the world - our faith. And who is the one who overcomes the world, but he who believes that Jesus is the Son of God?"
1 Jn 5:4-5 (NKJV)

We can carry victory in our hearts because of our faith in Jesus who has overcome the world for us. Our faith is not in our weakness but in the power of God.

So confront your fear with faith. Remember that through Jesus we confront a defeated enemy.

While you carry fear in your heart you are standing in the kingdom of darkness. You are giving Satan permission to hold you in bondage and to bring destruction and death into your life. To give reign to fear is to walk in disobedience and blessing will not flow in our lives no matter how much we pray to God for it. God will always honour the choice you make. Fear or faith!

Faith liberates us. Walking in fear can be a habit. So it means adopting new strategies in life so that we can walk in freedom. It takes effort and determination, but we are not alone when we choose to walk in obedience.

"I can do all things through Christ who strengthens me."
Php 4:13 (NKJV)

Fear or Faith. Futility or Freedom.
it's your choice – a choice we are all free to make.

## Trophies on the Billiard Room Wall

Just recently that wonderful iconic Australian comedy, "The Castle," was aired again on television. For me, one of the most endearing features of the film is that closely knitted bond of respect and love that exists between each of the family members.

When Sal Kerrigan serves up the evening meal, her husband Darryl, salutes her with, "And what do you call this darl?" "Chicken" comes the proud reply. Dessert is introduced with similar aplomb. "And what do you call this?" "Sponge cake" beams Sal with a smile from ear to ear.

Then there is the billiard room wall, that place of honour in the Kerrigan home for special family memories and mementos. Even their eldest son, languishing in prison after being involved in an armed robbery, is never far from their hearts and in spite of his sins is considered to be very much a part of the family.

Paul encourages us in Romans to express similar love and respect for one another:

"Be devoted to one another in brotherly love. Honour one another above yourselves." Rom 12:10 (NIV)

"We who are strong ought to consider the failings of the weak and not to please ourselves. Each of us should please his neighbour for his good, to build him up." Rom 15:1-2 (NIV)

How simple it is to give another a word of praise or encouragement. Praise pins a badge of honour on the recipient.

In honouring others we also honour ourselves. When Jesus was asked what was the greatest commandment he responded:

"Love the Lord your God with all your heart and with all your soul and with all your mind. This is the first and greatest

commandment. And the second is like it: 'Love your neighbour as yourself.' All the Law and the Prophets hang on these two commandments."
Mat 22:37-40 (NKJV)

Jesus reiterates this again in the Gospel of Matthew.

"So in everything, do to others what you would have them do to you, for this sums up the Law and the Prophets."
Mat 7:12 (NKJV)

How we see ourselves is reflected in how we treat others. Sowing and reaping is a spiritual principle that operates in the spiritual realm like gravity operates in the natural.

What goes up must come down;
what goes out must come back!

# The Gran Torino

If you haven't seen this Clint Eastwood movie, let me encourage you to do so. The opening scene of this film is that of Wal's wife's funeral - Wal is played by Clint Eastwood. The Catholic priest presiding starts his eulogy by proclaiming that death is both a bitter and a sweet experience. Bitter because loved ones are left in mourning but sweet because we know our deceased loved one is now going to be at peace with God.

Wal has little time for religion and when confronted later by the priest, who is a young man in his late twenties, he huffs dismissively that the priest in his celibate innocence actually knows very little about life or death. Ironically it is also Wal at this later stage of his life who still has a few things to learn about life. Wal is an elderly veteran of the Korean War and his once Polish neighbourhood has now largely become inhabited by Asians (Hmongs from Cambodia), for whom he has an innate prejudice. However Wal is not only coping with being alone and the cultural challenges of his neighbourhood but also his own mortality.

In amidst these challenges he finds himself unexpectedly drawn into friendship with a young Hmong teenage boy who he caught trying to steal his Gran Torino. It is in this friendship that Wal finds redemption for his own deep seated guilt which formed out of a fateful event that he was involved in during the Korean War.

This film has won standing ovations from movie goers in theatres around the world because it touches deep spiritual and emotional chords that resonate insight into the meaning of life and death and the importance of personal integrity. For me the following verse came to mind after I had seen it.

"Greater love has no one than this, that he lay down his life for his friends."
Jn 15:13 (NIV)

Who should our friends be, considering Jesus was described as a friend "of tax collectors and sinners" Lk 7:34 (NKJV)?

When I look back on my life as a young adult I see that I had a very idealistic black and white picture of the world. It was very judgemental and condemning of others who didn't measure up to "my" Christian way of thinking. Like Wal, I've had to learn to step over the boundaries of my prejudices with love and compassion instead of condemnation.

Jesus was always crossing the barriers of the accepted social norms of His time. Today we think of Him as a wonderful miracle wielding Saviour and forget that in His day He also had the reputation of one who ate with the marginalised tax collectors and prostitutes and stirred up trouble with the local authorities. Jesus never condoned sinful behaviour. When He spoke to the woman brought to Him after being caught in adultery, He didn't acknowledge her lifestyle choice as something that should be accepted as normal or even excused, He just forgave her.

But it didn't end there. He stood beside her in her sin and offered her a choice. A choice to take a new path in life that would lead her away from her sin (See Jn 8:4-11).

"Brethren, if a man is overtaken in any trespass, you who are spiritual restore such a one in a spirit of gentleness, considering yourself lest you also be tempted. Bear one another's burdens, and so fulfil the law of Christ."
Gal 6:1-2 (NKJV)

Like Wal, in order to take hold of our own redemption, we must first let go of our own prejudice and unforgiveness and offer the hand of friendship to those who have sinned against us. In order to bear each others burdens we must first lay down our stones. We need to come bearing compassion - not rocks of scorn.

# Looking Ghost Rider in the Eye

I happen to be a Nicholas Cage fan and Ghost Rider is just one of the latest in a whole series of movies that seem to be putting yet another of those wonderful Marvel comic characters and their epic adventures onto the silver screen. Perhaps those of us from the "baby boomer" generation will understand where I'm coming from. My husband grew up on the weekly instalments of those comics and just loved to immerse his young imagination in their marvellous adventures.

Nicholas Cage plays a character, called Johnny Blaze, a daredevil motorcyclist whom the devil tricks into selling his soul in return for the health of his father. Needless to say Johnny didn't see the small print in the contract that said although his father would recover, he would only have a short time to live regardless of his health!

Many years go by and just when Johnny's life seems to be turning around for good, the devil returns to claim his contract on Johnny

Blaze's soul, which bound him over whenever called upon to become the devil's bounty hunter of souls. So begins Johnny's transformation into the "Ghost Rider". He must now fulfil a contract for hunting down a thousand of the evilest souls whose evil deeds have bound them to the devil. The devil's son in opposition to his father is also seeking them in order to gain ultimate evil power for himself and consequently comes into conflict with Johnny.

Anyway in the course of fulfilling the contract, the Ghost Rider comes across a small time thug who is harassing a young woman for her valuables. The Ghost Rider grabs him. (Now the Ghost Rider is a blazing apparition with a furnace burning in each of the eye sockets of his skull.) The terrified thug now firmly retrained, looks into the eyes of the Ghost Rider who booms with a deep bass voice:

"Look into my eyes and see all the pain on all the faces of all the people you have ever harmed."

As the myriads of those tormented and hurt faces pass through the flames in the Ghost Rider's eye sockets, the thug turns to stone as he is pronounced guilty by the Ghost Rider.

At that moment, I felt a tremendous gratitude for God's Grace in my life for what Jesus had done for me. Like that thug I have hurt people both intentionally and unintentionally. Really I am no different. I might not have murdered anyone or snatched handbags from any old ladies but I know that I am not innocent of causing another's pain either. Like the thug, my sinful nature had bound me over to an eternity with Satan.

Because of God's Grace, so freely given, I know that I would have nothing to fear if the Ghost Rider ever looked into my eyes. He would see Jesus and pronounce me 'innocent'.

"If we say that we have no sin, we are deceiving ourselves, and the truth is not in us. If we confess our sins, He is faithful and righteous to forgive us our sins and to cleanse us from all unrighteousness." 1 Jn 1:8 (NIV)

When was the last time you really felt truly grateful for God's Grace in your life? Our gratitude is the well spring of joy for our lives. We can face life without guilt and fear of eternal condemnation. God's Grace empowers us to overcome all adversities and to successfully navigate through the messes we sometimes get ourselves into.

"For the wages of sin is death, but the gift of God is eternal life in Christ Jesus our Lord."
Rom 6:23 (NKJV)

# The Mines of Moria

In the early days of my youth, a group of us used to play in the bush in the foothills of Mount Coot-Tha in Brisbane. On one occasion we decided to crawl on our hands and knees with myself leading the way, through a very long and narrow drainage pipe underneath the newly constructed freeway. I look back now with the mind of an adult and wonder that we did not consider the possibility of meeting up with one of the venomous spiders and snakes that like to lurk in such dark places. Perhaps if we had, we might have missed out on a great adventure!

This reminded me of a scene in the "Lord of the Rings" where Gandalf's attempt to lead the members of the "Fellowship of the Ring" up over the Misty Mountains is thwarted with an avalanche. He is then forced to take a path that he had greatly resisted pursing, the path through the mountain, a path that leads through the mines of Moria (Moria means black chamber; a place of fear and foreboding).

There are times in our lives when circumstances press in on us and we might pray: "God, please take us around or take us over what lies in front of us". But God says: "You must go through."

Jesus faced a similar situation in the Garden of Gethsemane when he prayed:

"...Take this cup from me. Yet not what I will, but what you will"
Mk 14:36 (NIV)

Unlike his fellow travellers, Gandalf knew what lurked hidden in the primordial depths of the Mines of Moria. The inevitability of knowing that it waited for him... that he would have to face it.

Shadrach, Meshach and Abednego stared into the same inevitability as the heat of the furnace flamed on their faces. Yet after throwing them into the furnace, Nebuchadnezzar exclaimed:

"Look! I see four men walking around in the fire, unbound and unharmed. And the fourth looks like a son of the gods."
Dan 3:25 (NIV)

Gandalf faced the fiery demon, 'Balrog', on the bridge of Khaza-dum. Frodo and Aragorn watched on in anguished despair as the Balrog's fiery whip lashed out at Gandalf, toppling him into the darkness of the abyss below. But all of us "Lord of the Rings" fans know that this was not the end. Although Gandalf passed into darkness, out of time and thought, he ultimately defeated the Balrog and was resurrected to life again in Middle Earth as Gandalf the White.

There are many things we can fear in life. Rejection, loneliness, failure, succumbing to addictive habits or just simply making wrong decisions, are but a few that come to mind. Unfortunately when we give fear dominion over us, we will ultimately lose control of our lives. Unless we confront our fears, usually head on, we will always walk in defeat.

In order to know the resurrection power of Jesus in our lives we must bring death to our fears. Yes, there will be fighting. Yes, there will be pain. But ultimately there will be victory if we firmly hold on to our faith in the One who walks into the furnace with us.

When God next says to you, "You must go through", remember: Before there can be resurrection, there must be death!

"Whoever wants to save his life will lose it, but whoever loses his life for me will find it."
Mat 16:25 (NIV)

## Chapter Four:
### God moments can happen
# playing a game...

God Moments

# Confronting Diablo

My name is BrightStar and my Quest is to enter the Sanctuary of Chaos, break open the five seals and then destroy the arch demon, Diablo, who has one of the corrupted soul stones. I have fought my way through the Sanctuary of Chaos many times destroying the Pit Lords that breathe fire, demon knights, venomous slugs that spit poison and phantoms that suck the life out of you. But many times I have been unable to overcome the Master of Evil himself.

Many times I have released the seal that sets him free, with the ground trembling and quaking as he erupts forth from the central seal, his dark voice rumbling in my ears that I should prepare to meet my death.

Sending out his burning rings of fire, he moves towards me, I fight back but my life ebbs away and then its over: "BrightStar has been slain by Diablo" is emblazoned on my computer screen.

For months I have been trying to work out how to confront this demon and in frustration gave up for a few months, until recently when it came to me. I am weak in hand to hand combat. My power lies in my ability to control the elements of nature, fire, cold and lightning. I am easily overpowered if I come too close to my enemies but I have a mercenary who does that for me.

He engages demons one on one and cuts them down with his brandistock that poisons enemies, slowing them down which makes it easier to despatch them. However, my mercenary is no match for Diablo. This was one occasion I would have to do it for myself.

To overcome Diablo, I would have to get extremely close to him; I would have to wait for him right near the place where he would erupt from his seal. This was the very thing I had been so afraid of doing.

Previously in other game sessions I had stayed back not wanting to get close and fought him from a distance, often dying before I had a chance to do much. This time it was going to be different. This time I was going to overpower him before he had a chance to fight back. It would take courage and I must be prepared.

I filled my belt with the strongest mega sized health potions and armed myself. The moment he erupted I moved quickly forward blasting him with a freezing ice blast that immobilised him, preventing him from fighting back with his fire. I then got very close and used my lightning power to break down his defences twenty-five percent with each hit.

My heart was pounding as I used my last mega health potion. Diablo was still alive; this was it; one final ice blast. Then the ground erupted, balls of light shot up, "Diablo has been slain by BrightStar" was emblazoned on my computer screen.

Paul encouraged the Ephesians when facing difficulties to,

"Take up the full armour of God, that you may be able to resist in the evil day, and having done everything, to stand firm. Stand firm therefore, having girded your loins with Truth, and having put on the breastplate of righteousness, and having shod your feet with the preparation of the Gospel of Peace; in addition to all, taking up the shield of faith with which you will be able to extinguish all the flaming missiles of the evil one. And take the helmet of Salivation, and the sword of the Spirit, which is the word of God."
Eph 6:13-1 (NIV)

We all have Diablos to face. Situations that just fill us with fear and dread; those times when all we really want to do, is to run away and hide. Let someone else do the fighting. But no! The only way to overcome them is to meet them head on, up close and personal, just like my avatar in the computer game.

We need to stand firm in the face of our greatest fear because the power of the Holy Spirit, our Life source, goes with us into battle.

# Superheroes

One of the greatest attractions about playing computer games is that you can actually design your own avatar. In the virtual world, you can become the super hero you have always wanted to be in real life, with whatever powers you want. You can slay the monsters, rescue the prisoners and find the hidden treasures without leaving home or suffering any personal damage in the process.

Superheroes are inspiring to look up to and to live through. Every generation of children has there own particular assortment. Maybe for you it was Superman or Batman or even the Ninja Turtles.

When I was growing up, it was the characters of "Thunderbirds". Looking back at the programmes today through the eyes of an adult, the puppetry is awkward, the storylines are corny and the special effects are virtually non-existent. However, at the time, through the eyes of my childish imagination the characters were very real.

When the callsign, "Thunderbirds are go", came on the programme signalling the start of another mission, I was right there with the characters as though they were real flesh and blood. It was exciting. I lived through them the challenges of triumphing over the bad guys and revelled in their satisfaction that came with another mission successfully completed.

In our virtual world as avatars we can immerse ourselves in the fighting and overcoming the bad guys, but in the real world it can often be very different. Confronting the bad guys in real life is never an easy task and maybe that's why the idea of having a superhero coming to do it for us is so attractive. In the real world you can actually get hurt!

As we have just read in the previous story, God is calling us all to actively engage in conflict and confront the forces of evil, just like an avatar in a computer game.

There are times I'm sure when instead of rising to the challenge of donning the armour of a warrior, you have slunk away under the mantle of a worrier! Perhaps you have:

"Put on the whole mantle of the Worrier, so that when the day of evil comes you are immobilised. Then having done nothing taken up the helmet of futility, the belt of anxiety, the breastplate of depression, and with your feet fitted with gospel of fear prepared to flee. In addition to all this, you have taken up the shield of denial and with the sword of blame put to death all who would seek to give you wise counsel."

If you can relate to this - Be encouraged!

All is not lost. Admitting your weakness and failure can actually be the beginning place of your strength. After all, you are not alone when it comes to slinking away. You are in distinguished company. Peter might be one of the greatest apostles, but he is also known as one of the greatest slinkers of all time when faced with adversity!

The story of his denial of Christ, in spite of his promise not to do so, did not end there for Peter and neither does it have to for you. The last chapter of the Gospel of John was written so that all slinkers might know that there is hope for redemption.

Jesus came to Peter early one morning on the shores of the Sea of Galilee and called him again to battle. The coming of the Holy Spirit in the upper room on the Day of Pentecost transformed him from a slinker into a superhero.

"And He said to me, 'My grace is sufficient for you, for My strength is made perfect in weakness.' Therefore most gladly I will rather boast in my infirmities, that the power of Christ may rest upon me."
2 Cor 12:9 (NKJV)

Our strength lies in the superhero powers of the Holy Spirit. To become superheroes we need to wait in faith not run in fear.

"But those who wait on the LORD shall renew their strength; They shall mount up with wings like eagles, They shall run and not be weary, They shall walk and not faint."
Isa 40:31 (NKJV)

God Moments

God wants you as His avatar. He wants to live His Life through you!

"I have been crucified with Christ and I no longer live, but Christ lives in me. The life I live in the body, I live by faith in the Son of God, who loved me and gave himself for me."
Gal 2:20 (NIV)

# Band-Aids for a Broken Heart

When I first met my husband, he told me he was a financial planner. Now at the time, I didn't really know what that was, but I imagined it must be a boring sort of job like accountancy! Needless to say it was not love at first sight, especially as he also told me that he owned two little fluffy white dogs. (Not very manly I thought!)

We met at the squash courts. I had joined the club after my marriage fell apart in order to have some sort of social outlet as it was lonely at home on my own. Over the weeks we would spend time chatting in between games and so slowly got to know one another. As far as I was concerned we were friends and nothing more.

I used to literally throw myself into my games and would often bruise and abrade my knees in my earnest desperation to attack the ball. During one of these games when I abraded my knee it started to bleed, leaving little red markers on the court, a voice from the scorers balcony above the court suddenly called a halt to the game. The next thing I knew was that court door opened and there was my friend, kneeling down in front of me, applying Band-Aids to my wounded knee.

I looked into his eyes and my heart melted in response to such an expression of love and concern for my well-being. This act of kindness opened the door of love in my heart and so our friendship took on another dimension.

This is one of those very special moments in life that I look back on and just feel overwhelmed by the love of God. At that moment He opened my eyes to the wonderful man He had brought into my life;

with whom over the years I would begin to find a salve for my broken life and my broken heart. All brought about by some broken skin on my knee! Truly I could sing;

"He heals the brokenhearted and binds up their wounds."
Psa 147:3 (NKJV)

This incident also taught me something else about God. I had found love in the place I least expected it. In fact I found it in a place I was not even looking. What overwhelmed me was just how true God is to His Word. He knew what I needed and most of all He had fathomed the desires of my heart, even better than I had.

Left to my own devices I would have wandered off down another path wasting my time pursing what I thought was the best way of satisfying the desires of my heart. But No! God knew me better than I knew myself!

"Delight yourself also in the LORD, And He shall give you the desires of your heart. Commit your way to the LORD, trust also in Him, And He shall bring it to pass."
Psa 37:4-5 (NKJV)

God Moments

## Chapter Five:
**God moments can happen anytime, anywhere...**

## A Breakfast Bowl Moment

Breakfast is my favourite time of day. I usually get up an hour or two before my husband each morning. This is the time I have to myself; to potter about, read, meditate and just spend time with God before being engulfed in the business of the day.

Funnily enough, I would have to say that breakfast cereal is one of my favourite foods. To munch away, sipping on a hot tea with some reading material is simply the most heavenly way to break into the day. A few months ago in the course of my munching I looked down into my breakfast and there, swimming in the milk, was a weevil. On the side of the bowl was another of his companions, scurrying out from underneath the muesli flakes.

I stopped in mid munch with the thought; "Well it's not everyday you get a free living sacrifice in your breakfast bowl!"

I was immediately reminded of the passage in Romans where we are urged by Paul to be living sacrifices:

"Therefore, I urge you, brothers, in view of God's mercy, to offer your bodies as living sacrifices, holy and pleasing to God. This is your spiritual act of worship. Do not conform any longer to the pattern of this world, but be transformed by the renewing of your mind. Then you will be able to test and approve what God's will is, his good, pleasing and perfect will."
Rom 12:1-2 (NIV)

Then it suddenly dawned on me that the idea of a "living sacrifice" is such a dichotomy. Throughout the Bible and even in cultures where sacrifice is central to the worship ritual, whatever is sacrificed generally dies. Its life blood is poured out on the floor or into a bowl. In the Old Testament the Levites had a full-time job in the temple sacrificing all those lambs, goats, bulls and doves for the various sin and guilt offerings. The spilling of blood was central to the ritual of atonement and cleansing. Nothing survived and the meat was usually eaten by Levites. Even drink offerings were poured out and incense was burnt.

I thought of even more gruesome types of sacrifices, like the human sacrifices of the Aztecs, whose hearts were cut out as an offering to their sun god.

Surely nothing could survive a serious sacrifice because all sacrifices are broken and destroyed in some way. I know that if I had munched on my breakfast weevils that would have been the end of them. Crushed to death. Urgh! Now that's a disgusting thought!

How can a sacrifice continue to live? How could I live as sacrifice? I found this interesting verse in Psa 51:16 -17 (NIV):

"You do not delight in sacrifice, or I would bring it; you do not take pleasure in burnt offerings. The sacrifices of God are a broken spirit; a broken and contrite heart, O God, you will not despise.

Another dichotomy. God wants us to be broken but not to live in brokenness.

For whoever wants to save his life will lose it, but whoever loses his life for me will save it." Lk 9:24 (NIV)

Sacrifices are generally offered to appease or to please various deities so that blessing and abundance can flow into the worshippers' lives. In some cultures this was to ensure that the crops didn't fail or that the sun might continue to rise. When you think about the Jewish Temple, sacrifices were for very similar purposes. The Living God was angry with the human race because of their disobedience (sin); their refusal to accept His word as the Truth right back in the Garden of Eden. Lambs, bulls and goats were constantly being sacrificed as "sin" offerings. The Jewish priest transferred the guilt of the people by laying hands onto the animals before they were sacrificed to make atonement before God in order to appease His anger. (See Lev 4:29).

Yet it would seem that it is not the blood of lambs and bulls that

God really wants - it is us. It is our admission of disobedience (the broken and contrite heart) that God requires us to sacrifice. Paul says in the verse above that this is our true act of spiritual worship. Interesting because when you think of worship; you tend to think of people being joyful, singing and dancing before God, not about life blood shedding sacrifices.

It is not our physical death God is talking about here, it is our spiritual death. God wants to be first and foremost in our lives. Our sacrifice is ourselves, because in our own hearts we naturally believe that we are the most important people in the world (or gods in our own minds). Yet it is God who really is our life source, not ourselves. We sacrifice our independence for a total and complete dependence on God.

If we come before God in brokenness, our guilt is transferred to Jesus, the perfect "sin offering" made once and for all on our behalf.

God's wrath is coming on the world but if we make the sacrifice of ourselves, He has promised that we will not die in the fire of His judgement, but live. Our self-sufficiency and self-importance, these are the things that must die, so that resurrection life can become ours too as it did for Jesus.

Needless to say I let my breakfast weevils live. I didn't need their crushed bodies as protein supplements that day. Similarly God is willing to pardon us if we too are willing to become living sacrifices.

We are wanted alive not dead.

## A Shopping Trolley Moment

It is true - God hates divorce. (Mal 2:6). By divorce I don't mean just marriages but a breakdown in any kind of relationship. I had recently had some harsh words of disagreement with a fellow believer. We had parted without a resolution or an agreement being reached between us. The incident had been unpleasant and consequently over the ensuing weeks I continued to feel greatly troubled by this fall out. I had not known how to sort it out and so had done nothing.

Late one Saturday afternoon I realised that I needed a few essentials from the local shops and so hurried down as it was near closing time. Yes I made it, fifteen minutes before closing time. As I pushed my trolley around, I bumped into my estranged friend who was also making a last minute dash around the shops. There was no way I could avoid her; no time to make quick a foray into an adjacent aisle. She spotted me and came right up and spoke to me.

It was all very awkward. We chatted about the usual shallow daily stuff of life and then she brought up the incident of our disagreement. Now I had to address it! I just couldn't avoid it anymore. I felt hemmed in but when she spoke about what had happened, she expressed sorrow about all that had occurred.

We then found a connection between us again forged by mutual forgiveness. The unease in my heart dissipated.

A voice came over the shop intercom system, urging us to finalise our purchases. So we hugged and scurried off to fulfil our original shopping goals.

As I left the shops I said to God, "You did that on purpose, didn't You?" There was no reply, but I sensed a smug wide grin opening up on His face!

I was reminded then that I had not been alone in my distress. God was hurting too. Just like when you stub your toe, the whole body feels the pain, not just the toe. As joint members of the Body of the Christ, our dispute resulted in a more far reaching effect than I had even considered.

"...So in Christ we who are many form one body, and each
member belongs to all the others."
Rom 12:5 (NIV)

"Therefore each of you must put off falsehood and speak truthfully to his neighbour, for we are all members of one body... Be kind and compassionate to one another, forgiving each other, just as in
Christ God forgave you."
Eph 4:25, 32 (NIV)

God Moments

# When the Sparks Fly

As a small child I remember observing my father sharpening his tools on a grinder in the shed. It was a potentially hazardous task. My father wore face protection and we children were made to sit on the grass outside the workshop door. From our position of safety we could see the golden sparks fly and splinter off the blade of a metal tool as it was brought into contact with the whirring and rapidly spinning grinder wheel. Iron sharpening iron.

However, when the sparks fly in a relationship, can this ever be considered a good thing?

Experiencing conflict is a normal part of daily living. We live in a world of constant conflict and war. Within our society and even within Christian circles there is a tendency to consider all conflict as abnormal and something to be avoided at all costs. Perhaps you have occasionally heard some long standing married couples say: "We have the perfect marriage, we never argue and never have a cross word with each other". How can this be! Maybe they don't live in the same house or if they do – maybe they never talk to one another. Maybe their spouse is no longer even alive – that would make them dead easy to live with!

When a couple are first in love, everything is rosy, but the testing of that love will come when they have their first disagreement. Truly great love and truly great friendships are refined in the cauldron of conflict. The couple above may have a "peaceful marriage" but do they really have a "great love"?

In the time that we have been married, I would say that my husband and I have had many intense moments of fellowship. Yet we are still very much in love! Disagreement is never a pleasant experience, especially when the other person just simply will not concede that your point of view is the only fair and reasonable perspective that anyone with half a brain would see immediately as the absolute truth!!

Fighting for agreement is an underlying principle in our marriage relationship. The Bible has much to say about conflict and it can be seen as a positive construct in our lives.

"As iron sharpens iron, so one man sharpens another."
Prv 27:17 (NIV)

The suggestion that embracing friction can be positive and even necessary for personal and relational growth is rather challenging. It urges us to step outside our safety zones and enter into a potentially hazardous one where the sparks are flying.

Since I am a great advocate of reading Scripture within context, you will see that this verse comes immediately after a verse in Proverbs about contentious wives! These two verses make interesting companions for consideration.

"A quarrelsome wife is like a constant dripping on a rainy day; restraining her is like restraining the wind or grasping oil with the hand."
Prv 27: 16 (NIV)

After reading this verse you might have pity for her husband and admire his fortitude for living with such a disagreeable woman. However there is another angle on this. Maybe the husband is not really the innocent victim that we all like to feel so sorry for. Maybe the husband just withdrew from his wife because he was afraid to confront her and instead chose to live in intimidation. As a result of his choice to live in fear, the core issues in their relationship probably never got dealt with. Maybe she was quarrelsome because he never got around to fixing the dripping tap!

The quarrelsome wife is an example of poorly managed interpersonal conflict whereas the image of iron sharpening iron indicates how properly managed interpersonal conflict can be character building rather than soul destroying. Conflict that is ignored will become a persistent and festering sore within a relationship. Like a dripping tap that is not fixed so is the quarrelsome wife.

Conflict is not necessarily a bad thing;
it's just handled badly by most people.

## **Morning Walk**

Come
Weave your fingers into mine.

Let's feel the firm sand beneath our feet
And the lacy mirth of waves upon our toes.
Let the brassy breeze run fingers through our hair
And rub ruby roses into our laughing cheeks.

Let's call loudly to the day with the gulls
As they rise upon the salty air.
Let's talk of kings and things
And islands far away.

Let's fill the emptiness of now
With the fullness of each other.
Let's be friends forever and touch eternity
As we feel the fingertips of God upon our souls.

Kate Case 2003

## Chapter Six:
**God moments can happen**
# on your knees in prayer...

God Moments

# A Father's Heart

At my father's funeral, my aunt, who had looked after his affairs since my parents divorced following the onset of my father's illness, pointed out to me that he had no inheritance to leave me. Those were the only words she cared to speak to me that day. Regardless of whether or not my father should have had an earthly inheritance to pass onto his daughters, I knew she was wrong. He had left me something of priceless value.

I am the eldest of five daughters. On Sundays it was often difficult for my mother to come to church as she was constantly preoccupied caring for one of my infant siblings who seem to arrive in rapid succession, one after one another. The five of us were all born within a space of seven years. So on Sunday mornings, from a very young age, almost as soon as I could walk, I would usually go alone with my father to the "Morning Prayer" service in the little local convict hewn stone church where I was baptised.

Now this was a very high Anglican Church; no cry room, heaters, carpeted floors or padded seats here! As we sat in the front row of polished wooden pews, I would gaze up in awe at the early morning light streaming in through the stained glass windows which portrayed various saints in colourful magnificence. Morning Prayer was an unaccompanied service and the words of the liturgy were chanted. A great deal of this seemed to be done on our knees. Fortunately the kneelers were padded!

Quite an austere form of worship you might think, especially if you are more accustomed to the Pentecostal exuberant expression of joy.

I loved my father and as a small child spent many contented hours in his presence. He was an electrician and would often take me out with him on his jobs to give my mother a break. Probably wouldn't be allowed today with all the OH&S regulations we seem to have. I would play happily on the floor of a client's home while my father crawled around in their ceilings.

It was through being at his side on those church kneelers and through the repetitive words of creeds and prayers, that my father introduced me to his Father, the One in whose Presence he enjoyed spending time.

I did not know it at the time, but in a few short years that place of safety and comfort that was my fathers arms would be destroyed forever by his illness. I look back on those early years and am so grateful that while he had the time, my father spent it with me. As a result he has left me an inheritance more precious than pearls and more durable than gold; a faith in the Living God, who is a Friend to all who call upon Him as Saviour.

Spending time with our children is never wasted, even though as parents we are often pressed for time. We have only a few short years with them, to impart the precious knowledge and wisdom that they need to help them navigate the pitfalls of life by themselves.

"Train up a child in the way he should go, And when he is old he will not depart from it."
Prv 22:6 (NKJV)

My Father never preached to me about God and never forced me to go to church. I went with him gladly because I had a love relationship with him. I just loved being with my dad, wherever that might be.

Because of my father's heart for God I can now always say:

"I was glad when they said to me, 'Let us go into the house of the LORD.'"
Psa 122:1 (NKJV)

God Moments

# Falling Leaves

A gentle tap to my head;
a detour on your downward wend.
A summons from the Creators hand,
to spend some time in contemplative discourse
Consider anew the coming of our journeys end.

Your coursing to the ground
from verdant splendour cast;
A stark reminder, our earthly fabric, it does not last!

What worth in life, what place in death,
where can our meaning be found?
Show me, so that I can tell?
Are we that alike, yet so different,
Yet, each fashioned by the same Creator's hand.

Your crisp brown hue signifies a passing,
the soft and supple succulence of youth
so fast relinquished.
Yet in death you cry a final farewell:
Life is not extinguished!
There is purpose and meaning still.
You dive, so that life, can revive!

Once you adorned a poplars crown
bathed in summer dew,
nourished daily from a heavenly radiance,
suckled up above,
and lived in silent observation
of my footfall
far beneath.

Now here's the crunch - your destiny,
it lies underfoot in mulch!

Mine is glory bound
when I shed this earthy frame,
to rise up high,
to join the Son's eternal reign.
No time for grieving.
In both our leavings
we will meet and greet
the New Life, that each of us, is receiving.

Kate Case 2011

God Moments

## Chapter Seven:
**God moments can arrive**
# in the post...

## Fridge Door Art

Some time ago we received a large envelope in the mail from my husband's granddaughter. We knew it was from her because it was addressed to Grandad and Granny Kate and when we opened it all sorts of glitter and sparkles dropped out. Inside were three beautiful hand paintings done in vibrant pinks, purples and greens and covered in decorations and glitter.

So lovely were the pictures that they now adorn our fridge door for all to admire. How special it was to have such a simple gift sent to us. It brought so much pleasure to our hearts and in return drew out of us a loving response. It's not that we didn't already love her, but it was her simple gift that drew out our love for her, so much so that we were moved to send her something in return - something we knew she would just love and be overjoyed to receive.

I pondered at the time how it must be the same for our Heavenly Father. How it must thrill His heart with joy when His children come into his presence bringing their simple gifts of love rather than just fronting up to Him and proceeding to run through their shopping lists of needs.

God's love for us is unquestionable and so is His desire to provide for our needs. But how much more freely must His love flow into our lives when we just come to Him with thankfulness and love in our hearts. By doing so we are showing a longing to dwell in God's presence and not just a desire to receive His presents!

How much more will His blessing flow into our lives and how much more easily will we find all our needs met by His abundant love in return when we come to Him with our love gifts.

"Shout joyfully to the LORD, all the earth. Serve the LORD with gladness; Come before Him with joyful singing. Know that the LORD Himself is God; It is He who has made us, and not we ourselves; We are His people and the sheep of His pasture. Enter His gates with thanksgiving, And His courts with praise.

Give thanks to Him; bless His name. For the LORD is good;
His loving kindness is everlasting, And His faithfulness
to all generations."
Psa 100:1-5 (NIV)

Anytime of day is good time to come into God's presence with praise. We don't have to store it all up for the Sunday worship service in church. We can puncture our days with mini praise events. It's all part of the spontaneity of sharing within a love relationship. My husband and I often interrupt each other's days just to share stuff about the happenings in our immediate lives.

Taking time for mini praise events keeps our daily dialogue open with God. When we praise we enter into that holy place where God dwells. A place where, when He speaks to us, we will readily hear His voice.

## Christmas Card Contemplation

Almost everybody loves to receive birthday cards. They are reminders to the recipient of that momentous event that began it all - their birth. When you think about it, Christmas is really just a big birthday celebration - Jesus' birthday. The sending of cards is also very much a part of it except we send them to each other, not to Jesus. Maybe that's appropriate.

The nativity scene would be by far the most popular depiction on the cards. Baby Jesus lying in His manger with His adoring mother, Mary, looking on, surrounded by animals, shepherds and wise men. Jesus is at the centre of everyone's attention. Rightly so. It was a momentous event for God to confine His glory within a human frame and to walk as a man in the place of Adam's exile. That place of weeds and thistles where birth always ends in death and the hopes of mothers who look upon the faces of their newborns infants with such expectant promise, are dashed upon the rocks of life's hard knocks.

# God Moments

Mary was probably no different to any other mother when she looked into the tiny newborn face of her son. She probably recalled the words spoken to her by the angel Gabriel and imagined her son being a great leader of her people, a king even, sitting in splendour on a throne. Such thoughts would only have been affirmed by the lavish abundance of the gifts arrayed at his feet by the strange Wise Men from the east. She would not have been contemplating his death in those first few moments of wonder.

How little did Mary understand then, that the moment God chose to become her son was the moment He chose to die. Eternity had just subjected itself to time and the clock was ticking for humanity.

If you have seen the film "Alien" you will know that at the end of the film the only way for Ripley to survive and to kill the evil infesting the space craft was to deploy the "self-destruct" mechanism. Lights flash, sirens whirr and a voice comes over the intercom; "Warning! This craft is about to be destroyed. You have ten minutes to make it to a place of safety."

God's plan from the beginning has always been to destroy evil. Satan was forewarned in the Garden when Adam and Eve became the offspring of rebellion.

"And I will put enmity between you and the woman, and between your offspring and hers; he will crush your head and you will strike his heel."
Gen 3:15 (NIV)

Jesus did indeed come to die. His sole purpose for coming was to die! He came so that eternity could reclaim time and to bring Adam home from exile.

But God had an escape plan to save humanity from the coming destruction and it came in the form of a newborn child. He came so that humanity could find a place of safety in his death.

"... your life is now hidden with Christ in God."
Col 3:3 (NIV)

# Tiny Hands

As I gaze upon your tiny face,
I marvel at what you've sacrificed for human grace.
From glory infinite you stepped aside
and in a child's humble frame became confined.
Such tiny hands encircle your mother's finger
as you suckle in her warm embrace.
Soon as a man you'll tread this rugged earthly terrain

These tiny hands will touch a lepers fetid skin
and make him clean.
These tiny hands will grasp the fury of a storm
and its violence pacify.
These tiny hands will touch the cold and torpid corpse
of a widow's only son infusing warmth and life.
These tiny hands will break the bread
and fish of a small boy's lunch so a multitude can feed.
These tiny hands will in agony be bound,
and in pain grimace upon a cross.

For what gain may I ask did You give all to suffer such loss?
These tiny hands have shown me the way,
That death may die and eternal Life be there for all to gain.
These tiny hands bid me come and do the same.

Kate Case 2001

God Moments

## Chapter Eight:
### God moments can happen when you're
# cooking up a storm...

God Moments

# Beans on Toast

Sunday evenings are special for us. It's the one day of the week when I really don't have to think too much about preparing the evening meal. We like to take Sunday afternoons easy, often spending them reading the newspaper, just taking time out. It's pleasant after a busy week, just to relax and not be compelled to do anything remotely resembling work.

So in keeping with the mood, Sunday evenings are welcomed in with beans on toast accompanied by some bacon (low fat, of course) and eggs on the side. Very easy to prepare and very enjoyable. There's always plenty to share should anyone happen to drop by to join us.

I am reminded of another family that Jesus visited for an evening meal:

"Now as they were travelling along, He entered a certain village; and a woman named Martha welcomed Him into her home. And she had a sister called Mary, who moreover was listening to the Lord's word, seated at His feet.

But Martha was distracted with all her preparations; and she came up to Him, and said, "Lord, do You not care that my sister has left me to do all the serving alone? Then tell her to help me."

But the Lord answered and said to her, "Martha, Martha, you are worried and bothered about so many things; but only a few things are necessary, really only one, for Mary has
chosen the good part, which shall not be taken away from her."
Lk 10:38-42 (NKJV)

Who really was the focus of Martha's attention? It certainly was not Jesus. Here she is getting hot and bothered and actually ignoring the guest she was trying to impress.

I reckon Jesus would have been happy with beans on toast, just so that He could spend some carefree time hanging out with His friends. Killing the fatted calf and the multi-course banquet Martha had in mind was not what Jesus meant when He called by and asked if He could spend some time with His friends.

How often do we get carried away with all our programmes for God and think that all the fuss we make with our preparations and efforts should somehow impress Him. When programmes and preparations take precedence over spending time in the presence of God we have totally missed the point.

Taking time to hang out with God and our fellow members of the Body of Christ is never wasted. These times bring refreshment and joy and sustain us through times when our efforts are required. The simple things in life are often the best.

## Guess Who's Coming to Dinner

Christmas lunch is a very central part of our Christmas festivities. Judging by the queues at the check outs in Woolies on Christmas Eve, we're not the only ones. There are generally trolleys and baskets brimming with all sorts of goodies and delicacies.

One one occasion we had twelve people around our table. Actually thirteen, if you count Jesus. Yes, I reckon Jesus was there too, because if you have read the New Testament, you will see that Jesus enjoyed a good feed and a glass of wine on many occasions. Just take a moment to consider how many of Jesus' recorded social interactions with people are actually centred around a shared meal. In fact it was the Jewish food laws which the Pharisees constantly accused Him of disregarding.

"But the Pharisees and the teachers of the law muttered, 'This man welcomes sinners and eats with them.'"
Lk 15:2 (NIV)

It was at a festive meal together before Jesus' betrayal and death that He said this to His disciples.

"When the hour came, Jesus and his apostles reclined at the table. And he said to them, 'I have eagerly desired to eat this Passover with you before I suffer. For I tell you, I will not eat it again until it finds fulfilment in the kingdom of God.' After taking the cup, he gave thanks and said, 'Take this and divide it among you. For I tell you I will not drink again of the fruit of the vine until the kingdom of God comes.'"
Lk 22:14-18 (NIV)

So what does Jesus actually mean by the Kingdom of God? Well, His disciples asked Him the same question and this was His answer:

"The kingdom of heaven is like a king who prepared a wedding banquet for his son...."
Mat 22:2 (NIV)

You know the story. He asked many to come but they refused, so he sent His servants out into byways and the fields and invited all who would come. When the banquet was ready to begin this is what happened:

"But when the king came in to see the guests, he noticed a man there who was not wearing wedding clothes. 'Friend,' he asked, 'how did you get in here without wedding clothes?'
The man was speechless. Then the king told the attendants, 'Tie him hand and foot, and throw him outside, into the darkness, where there will be weeping and gnashing of teeth.' For many are invited, but few are chosen."
Mat 22:11-14 (NIV)

Well somehow I don't think we'll be sitting around eating "philly" on crackers in heaven! Jesus was very much into enjoying life, for He said:

"I came that you might have life and have it abundantly."
Jn 10:10 (NIV)

There will be feasting and celebration in eternity.

Yet are you fully prepared for the banquet prepared in eternity? Who would turn up to a wedding in their old gardening T-shirt and threadbare shorts? Do you have your wedding clothes? First you must put off your old clothes in order to be garbed with the fine raiment, fit for such a celebration.

"For all of you who were baptised into Christ have clothed yourselves with Christ."
Gal 3:27 (NIV)

In spite of all the New Years' resolutions that you might make; to drink less, eat less, exercise more, to be nice to the in-laws (or whatever), you cannot enjoy a new life without first putting off our old life!
   You cannot experience abundant life without experiencing the giver of abundant life.

Jesus really is the Life of the party!

# A Little Faith Cooking

My husband loves dumplings. When he first met me he didn't actually believe I could cook. Not surprising as my first attempts to impress failed miserably. We joke now about my "apple bumble," the wanna be apple strudel that fell apart and my "crunchy lasagne" that didn't quite pass the munch test.

Dumplings are rather simple to make but can be a bit tricky to cook correctly. I was determined after several failed attempts that I was going to get it right. It was going to work out because I was going to get God involved. After all, doesn't it say in the Bible that all things are possible for him who has faith in God and that faith as small as mustard seed can move a mountain? So it shouldn't be too difficult with a little bit of faith to get God to cook a few dumplings properly!

I put all the raw ingredients together in bowl, a whole egg still in its shell, a cup with some water, some flour and an unopened box of suet. I bowed in my most prayerful attitude before God and said:

"Here is my problem, cooking dumplings. You know how often I've failed at this, so I'm handing it all over to You this time. I have faith in you God that you can do this for me. I am speaking with faith into this bowl. I am believing for a miracle here. I cast out all doubt and negative thoughts. I speak against all the powers of anti-cooking that seek to enter my kitchen. In You alone do I trust. In You alone do I put all my faith. Amen."

Having done my part in prayer, I then left the kitchen to give God some space while He worked on my problem.

I came back into the kitchen after the allotted cooking time for dumplings. What! Everything was just as I had left it. Can't God read instructions? They were all there for Him to follow. Maybe I should have prayed and fasted before asking. Maybe that was why my faith in God wasn't working. Sound familiar? How often do we just dump our problems on God and walk away "in faith", expecting nothing short of a miraculous fix!

How do you see God? The great "Mr Fixit" who lives in the sky or as a trusted Friend who will walk alongside you into the stuff of life?

Adam and Eve were given the Garden of Eden to care for by God (See Genesis 3). I'm sure when God came to walk with them in the cool of the evening at the end of each day, He would discuss with them any problems they might have encountered during the day. I could envisage that together they would have come up with workable solutions; the implementation of which would always have been the responsibility of Adam and Eve.

Having faith in God is not about manipulating God to fix our problems for us; it's about having the courage and the wisdom to do stuff for ourselves!

Think about it: When Jesus berated his disciples for not having enough faith it was generally in the context of them being too afraid to actively step out and do something He was calling them to do. Consider also Peter who initially stepped out in faith to walk on the water towards Jesus but started sinking after becoming afraid when he focused on the sea around him instead of Jesus.

Faith calls us to journey forward with God not to stand staring into space while waiting for God to get His act together and move in our direction.

Fear fixates on the problems but faith focuses on the possibilities.

There is nothing wrong with asking God for help with our problems, I often seek His help, sometimes for the smallest things. The miracle is that He often responds with a suggestion that just blows my mind and what's more works when I put it into action.

Want to know the best way to cook dumplings? Follow the instructions ...exactly!

If you want life to work out, work it out with God and follow the instructions ...exactly!

God Moments

Chapter Nine:
**God moments can happen when you're**
**forlorn in sheer frustration...**

# Through the Looking Glass

I have been wearing glasses since I was three years of age. They are so much a part of my face that I don't think about them until I literally see spots before my eyes and realise its time to clean them. And wow – what a difference it makes! The crisp brightness to the world floods in on me, replacing the hazy gloom that I had gradually become accustomed to.

How we see life depends on how we brings its events into focus.

David in the Old Testament spent many years before he became king, fleeing from Saul who was determined to kill him. How did David respond during such times of desperation? Where was his focus?

"One thing I ask of the Lord, this is what I seek: That I may dwell in the house of the Lord all the days of my life, To gaze upon the beauty of the Lord and to seek him in his temple. For in the day of trouble he will keep me safe in his dwelling; He will hide me in the shelter of his tabernacle and set me high upon a rock."
Psa 27:4-5 (NIV)

When things get tough, when disappointment comes yet again, when things go wrong just when we thought they were going so right at last, where is the focus of our faith?

Instead of becoming an embittered and angry man, David used his difficult circumstances as a focal point for his faith in God. Many of his greatest Psalms were written during his time as a fugitive. It was because of his faith in God and his unwavering assurance of God's abiding presence that David was able to endure.

We are never more alone than when we focus only on ourselves and our problems.

When we focus our problems through God's promises we will bring to light the crisp reality of the hope and security we have because the Living God is walking beside us as a Friend.

Jesus said:

"I have told you these things, so that in me you may have peace. In this world you will have trouble. But take heart! I have overcome the world."
Jn:16:33 (NIV)

God wants us to be at peace not in pieces. No problem is too big when you have the Creator of the universe helping you fit the pieces into place.

# Unlocking God's Blessing

Some weeks ago my husband and I found ourselves locked out of the house. Each of us had thought the other had the keys before locking and closing the front door. After circumnavigating the house checking for open windows (of which there were none), my husband decided to get a ladder and climb onto the roof. We have a two storey house, a highset as they call them here in Queensland. The view from up on the roof, overlooking Moreton Bay, is magnificent. Anyway, after removing a number of roof tiles, and disappearing into the ceiling he finally appeared on the inside of the front door with the keys!

We were determined that this should not happen again and decided to get some keys cut that we could hide in a place where they could be easily retrieved should we become locked out again.

Simple enough strategy, except that the keys we got cut would not open the front door. They looked very similar to the originals but on closer inspection you could see some minor inconsistencies. It actually took another two attempts to get the keys correctly cut so that we could open the front door with them.

Jesus said He came that we might have an abundance of life (Jn 10:10). The Bible is full of God's promises of blessing (2 Pet 1:4) but,

I think many of us struggle with receiving God's blessing into our lives. We can even become disheartened and think that God is mean spirited. We don't really need to strive to convince God to bless us. The problem lies with us and our inability to access his blessings.

It all comes down to having the correct key to open the door to the blessing we are seeking to access. Many of us struggle because we are using counterfeit keys, just like the ones we got cut that wouldn't open the door. So what are the correct keys?

"Trust in the Lord with all your heart, and do not lean on your own understanding. In all your ways acknowledge Him, and He will make your paths straight. Do not be wise in your own eyes; fear the Lord and turn away from evil. It will be healing to your body, and refreshment to your bones.

Honour the Lord from your wealth, and from the first of all your produce; so your barns will be filled with plenty, and your vats will overflow with new wine. My son, do not reject the discipline of the Lord, or loathe His reproof, for whom the Lord loves He reproves, even as a father, the son in whom he delights."
Prv 3:5-12 (NIV)

These are the keys to having a correct attitude of heart. In order to unlock God's blessing we have to be in the place where Gods blessing is – and that is walking with God. Then the floodgates will open and blessing will flow into our lives.

Sometimes in order for us to receive God's blessing, God has to make some changes in our lives as the last two verses in the above passage indicate. So don't be surprised when you ask to be blessed, things sometimes get tougher instead of better. Maybe God needs to deal with some areas in your life first where you are not really walking in obedience and have not learnt to trust Him in yet.

Honour God and He will bless you. Dishonour God with your life, your words, your attitude, or withhold praise and worship from God, and God's blessing will not flow in your life.

Unlocking God's blessing is much easier to achieve when you have the correct keys!

# A Miracle Moment

In 2005, my husband suffered from a frozen shoulder. This is a very painful and incapacitating affliction. However, at the time, none of the medical professionals were entirely sure of the diagnosis. As the pain got worse he had to give up playing squash. He could not raise his left arm in the air or even lace his belt into his trousers. (An interesting dilemma when I was not there to help!)

This disease process generally affects women more than men and roughly runs an eighteen month course consisting of six months of getting worse, six months of agony and six months of getting better! All manner of alternative therapies, pills and potions seemed to do little to alter its course.

In order to definitively confirm a diagnosis he was eventually referred to an orthopaedic surgeon. An anaesthetic to further investigate and to inject steroids into the joint was proposed. It was at this juncture I raised some concerns as a week or so previous to this I had come home from shopping to find my husband sitting sucking on his nitro spray, exhausted after mowing the lawn.

In view of my husband's prior history of a heart attack several years earlier, the orthopaedic surgeon recommended we obtain a referral from our local doctor to a cardiovascular specialist for further investigations.

A referral letter was obtained on the following Saturday from our local GP. This was the middle of November and in just under four weeks we were booked on a flight to Europe to visit my husband's family in England.

I phoned the cardiovascular specialist's surgery first thing on the following Monday. She explained that he would be lucky to get an appointment before the end of January the following year. Rather than hanging up right there and then, I felt strongly prompted to ask her if she had any cancellations. She said, "Hang on, I'll have a look". She came back on the phone and said; "We have one today at 11.00am. Can you come now?"

Two days later my husband received two stents into his coronary arteries and three weeks later he was skiing in Austria. The pain in his shoulder was much better as well.

If my husband had received surgery a few days later than when he did, we would not have been able to fly. We would have had to cancel our trip as flying within three weeks of this type of procedure is not permitted.

For me, this whole event was miraculous and even today I get goose bumps just thinking about it.

This was not one of those "get laid on with hands" instantaneous healings or one of those spectacular types of miracles that people seem to hang out for. There was no lightning bolt from heaven. No, it was something much more special. This was the power and authority of God manifesting in the midst of my daily life struggles.

Through this experience I came to realise just how much God is there in the midst of my stuff. Closer than my next breath. I did not have to pray and fast or stand on my head to bring forth His Presence. No, He is just always there. Always caring. And always involved.

"The LORD himself goes before you and will be with you;
he will never leave you nor forsake you. Do not be afraid;
do not be discouraged."
Deut 30:8 (NIV)

## Chapter Ten:
**God moments can happen when you're**
# crying out in desperation...

# God's Wrecking Ball

Some years ago I was going through some difficult times when my previous marriage was ending and my life as I knew it was unravelling. I felt very desolate and alone. I cried out to God in my pain, trying to make sense of it all. God came near to me and in the solitude of my anguish, gave me a vision of a large wrecking ball smashing into the side of a building, demolishing the entire structure.

God seemed to be saying to me, "Kate, you have built these structures in your life but they are not fit for habitation. I am going to totally destroy your life as you know it."

"Well, that's cheery!" I thought. "Here I am in pain and God, you're just promising me... More pain!"

The hours, weeks and months went by as I languished in the deep darkness of depression where I could see no light at the end of the tunnel. Periodically I cried out to God, "Have you finished wrecking my life yet?" I was anxious to escape my world of pain but the soft answer that would come back to me was, "Not yet Kate".

Thankfully now I'm in the re-construction phase of my life. I can now look back on those dark times and see them as a necessary, albeit painful experience, and although I felt so utterly alone, God really was there. At the beginning of the dark times I had also received a reminder from God that when he sent his children into exile he also sent them with a promise of restoration. Exile was only ever for a predetermined time.

God is like that. He wants us to have hope, not despair, even in the face of disaster. He only allows destruction so that there can be re-construction and exile so that there can be reconciliation.

We come to God as we are. While He loves and accepts us as we are, we really come as condemned dwelling places. When we invite God into our lives, we are inviting in a furnace like refining fire, and a violent rushing wind.

Individually and corporately we are meant to be the dwelling place of God.

"Jesus answered and said to him, 'If anyone loves Me, he will keep My word; and My Father will love him, and We will come to him, and make Our home with him.'"
Jn 14:23 (NIV)

Yes, we are to be God's home. Not just a lowly two up two down with creaky floorboards and dodgy plumbing, but a home of ornate beauty and palatial magnificence on the scale of Buckingham Palace. Nothing else would be fit for our King and Creator.

Yet we come to God with structures in our lives built out of our sinful behaviours and founded on half truths and lies. These have often taken years to fabricate. Minor repairs will not cover up the defects in our habits and ways of thinking while leaving the corrupt foundations intact. No, they all must be demolished and cast into the fire or blown away in the cyclonic wind of the Holy Spirit.

So if you are going through tough times, don't be too quick to blame Satan. If you have asked the Holy Spirit to come and dwell in your life maybe He is just making Himself a home!

# The Guilt Trap

Anyone who has been through divorce or the brokenness of a relationship often carries a deep seated sense of rejection and a lack of self worth. I know that was certainly the case for me. The very fact that as a Christian, I was staring divorce in the face seemed to make it worse, as it had been my deep seated conviction that believers just did not get divorced – ever. It was an unforgivable sin. It was contemptible.

Not once have I ever heard anyone preach on how to have a good divorce! Yet over the years I have heard countless sermons on how to have a good Christian marriage and how it was our solemn duty as believers to uphold it at all costs against a worldly onslaught of temptation and vice. Yet here was mine, broken and in irreconcilable pieces.

I know I am not alone with my struggles with guilt and regret over how things in life have turned out. Many people struggle with them, especially those whose actions have inadvertently caused irreparable damage to others.

Guilt is a by-product of disobedience. It comes when we know we have done something wrong and broken the law. We live in fear of punishment and rejection and maybe even death as direct consequence of our actions. It is understandable then that a guilty person will often seek to cover up their wrong doing and when confronted will deny it or deflect the blame onto someone else.

We squirm under our guilt, not willing to face ourselves or anyone else. We feel trapped by it; held fast like a rabbit in a snare.

I remember an occasion when both my children were very young and were playing together in the next room. My son came to me in tears. There in the middle of his back was a deeply imprinted set of teeth marks. I questioned my daughter about this and shaking her head, she denied all knowledge of it!

It was guilt that kept Adam and Eve from approaching God after they had chosen to believe the serpent's words instead of God in the Garden of Eden. They used to always go for walks in the cool of the evening with God but when He called to them that fateful day, they remained hidden in shame in the bushes, separated from God. How God's heart must have ached knowing that the intimate relationship they had shared was now destroyed. What followed was denial, blame deflection and ultimately banishment for Adam and Eve.

Struggling with guilt can lead to physical and emotional distress as David knew only too well when he wrote these words after his affair with Bathsheba:

"When I kept silent, my bones wasted away through my groaning all day long. For day and night your hand was heavy upon me; my strength was sapped as in the heat of summer. Then I acknowledged my sin to you and did not cover up my iniquity. I said, 'I will confess my transgressions to the LORD - and you

forgave the guilt of my sin."
Psa 32:3-5 (NIV)

I wonder how different things might have been if Adam and Eve had rushed up to God when he first called them and just admitted what they had done? I would have loved my daughter just to have openly admitted to me "Yes, that is my dental impression on my brother's back!" I would have inwardly rejoiced.

Hanging onto guilt leads us on a path away from God and the truth. It estranges us from God and one another. Our faith turns to fear. We become afraid of God. Afraid of punishment. Afraid of rejection.

Hanging onto guilt is a refusal to receive God's forgiveness; it is to deny the power of the sacrifice of Jesus on the Cross. To consider ourselves or anyone else unworthy of God's forgiveness is to call God a liar. It is nothing less than open rebellion.

God is the greatest fixer of all time. There is nothing that is broken that cannot be mended or restored if we bring it to Him instead of holding onto it. David knew this and we can know it too.

Admitting our guilt may be the hardest thing to do but it is easiest in the long run.

"If we confess our sins, God is faithful enough to forgive our sins and to purify [cleanse] us from all unrighteousness."
1 Jn 1:9 (NIV)

We have no basis for being afraid of God. God has made a way for it to be safe to come into His Presence without fear of rejection or going to hell. Remember that on Good Friday the curtain surrounding the Holy of Holies in the Jewish temple in Jerusalem was torn in two from bottom to top. The way into the Presence of God was now clear for everyone.

Christ laid down his life for us and took the full brunt of God's anger for our wrong doing on Himself. He suffered the ultimate rejection by God so that we would never again have to be afraid of coming into God's presence. For those who accept the forgiveness of God into their lives, God's presence is a safe place.

Our guilt belongs with Jesus, nailed to the cross.

Nobody is unworthy of forgiveness; there is no wrong that cannot be forgiven. There is no person that cannot be restored to a relationship with God if they are willing to come before Him and openly confess their mistakes.

Yes I had failed but I needed to take responsibly for my role in that failure just like David ultimately did for his failures. Yes there are still consequences for our wrong doing but being separated from the love of God should not be one of them. David's son died. My life and relationships did fall apart and at the time of writing that estrangement from family still exists.

Yet God did give David another son and I am now very happily re-married.

God never wanted me to stay in my state of guilt and we do a great disservice to fellow believers when we burden them with guilt and fear of rejection for their failures before God.

Confession gives God permission to deal with the root cause of our failures - ourselves. Like Adam and Eve, it is our refusal to face our guilt and not our acceptance of it that will ultimately lead to rejection and estrangement from God.

Confession springs opens the guilt trap and forgiveness pulls us free.

# **Light Up Your Life**

I lived in England for a number of years after I was first married. Winter time there is often a bit gloomy and depressing. Daylight comes around ten o'clock in the morning and disappears around three o'clock in the afternoon and if you're very lucky actual sunshine will appear for about ten minutes every few days! During one particularly gloomy winter the whole country went without any sign of sunshine or light for a whole two weeks. At the end of this period a disturbing report came over the radio saying that there had been a significant rise in the suicide rate during this time.

There was a time in my life many years after this, when I succumbed to suicidal depression myself. It was a very dark and lonely time for me and despite the encouragement of well-meaning friends I could not see any light at the end of the tunnel. Just total blackness.

In the middle of the English winter there is Christmas. Christmas is a magical time in England and since then for me, Christmas in Australia has never been quite the same. You see, in England, in the evenings all the Christmas lights would come on inside the shop windows, in the streets and inside people's homes. The world was no longer gloomy, just magical with multitudes of sparkling iridescent lights. In England there's actually snow on the ground, not just on the Christmas cards. Christmas is spent in front of a blazing open fire, not in the blazing heat in front of a fan.

In the northern hemisphere Christmas comes at the time of year when the shortest day occurs, the winter solstice, which actually falls on the twenty-first of December. This was the time when a pagan festival occurred to encourage the sun to come back again, to bring light back into a world that was in darkness.

When recounting the start of Jesus' ministry, Matthew wrote this in his gospel:

"The people who were sitting in darkness saw a great light, and to those who were sitting in the land and shadow of death,
upon them a light dawned."
Mat 4:16 (NIV)

Now that place of darkness sounds just like England in winter and just like the place where I was languishing in depression.

Light is a central theme of the Bible. God is described as being wrapped in light. (Psa 104:2) In Genesis, God's first act of creation was to separate the light from the darkness (Gen 1:3). God's Word is described as, "a lamp to my feet, and a light to my path" (Psa 119:105 NKJV).

Darkness can be defined as a place where God's presence is absent. I believe that Hell, rather than being a place of fire and brimstone as portrayed in popular belief, is a place of eternal darkness and solitude, just like that place described in the Bible where there is weeping and gnashing of teeth (Mat 8:12).

Moving into God's light or staying in the darkness: the choice really is ours to make. A choice that determines our eternal destination. While darkness is not God's intended destination for you and me, he will not force us to choose.

Walking in the light with Jesus is by invitation, not conscription.

At the darkest point of my depression, just before I was about to be admitted to hospital, Jesus came to me in a vision and asked me to come and walk with Him in the Garden. There was a place of great peace and beauty. After taking His hand and spending time with Him there, I was no longer afraid. I had come to a point in my illness where holding onto my faith in God had become very difficult, but now I knew there was hope.

That day was a turning point for me. I could have chosen to wallow in self pity and stay in my dark hole but when I reached out to take hold of God's outstretched hand, a light became visible at the end of the tunnel.

We don't drive the darkness out; we dispel the darkness by turning on the light.

Each Christmas, after some mild nagging from myself, my husband finally puts up some Christmas lights, including a flashing star in our front window! We have lots of lights and they make a brilliant display, but it is our choice whether or not to put them up. If we don't, then the end of the street will just stay gloomy after dark. (Hurrah you might say, less local traffic congestion from after dark sightseers!)

Why continue to live a life in darkness where there is fear and death; where the future is without hope and the present promises no fulfilment beyond the moment?

We need to find and flick the switch on God's Christmas light; a light that will permeate us with the hope eternal life.

After all, there will only ever be eternal darkness without it.

God Moments

# **Feathers**

"He will cover you with His feathers
and under His wings you will find refuge" Psa 91:4 (NIV)

They said:
At the end of the tunnel there is light
But all I see is dead of night
The grip of pain
It binds me tight

As I lay me down to sleep
Cover me with your feathers
Lord, you know, my soul it weeps

They said:
The Lord will not burden you
With more than you can bear
What would they know?
They don't walk daily in despair

As I close my eyes tonight
Cover me with your feathers
Lord, and just hold me tight

They said:
All things work towards good
For those who love the Lord
But they don't know the road I travel
Or my struggle with daily moving forward

As the darkness closes all around
Cover me with your feathers
Lord, take me to that place where peace is found.

They said:
Don't fear, just have faith in God
Leave it there, He'll work it out.
All I want to do is in anger shout
It's not fair, why have You brought me here
Don't You care?

As I toss and turn
Cover me with your feathers
Lord, give me the answers that I yearn

But they didn't know:
That crying through the night must endureth
Before the morning joy can be brought forth
That the banquet just for myself prepared
Can only be reached though the shadowy vale of death
That the blooming of the summer rose
Can only come with the melting of the winter snows

As I lay me down all forlorn
Cover me with your feathers
Lord, I know You'll walk with me into the dawn

Kate Case 2010

# **Unplugged**

In the mid nineties I moved up to Tamworth from Sydney with my family and we eventually settled on a five acre block up in the hills just north of Tamworth. Apart from the wonderful view, when you walked outside at night it was completely dark, especially when there was no moonlight. There are no streetlights and you can look up at the sky and appreciate the brilliance of the Milky Way. Occasionally there would be quite violent electrical storms and we would be plunged into power blackouts for a number of hours.

Lightning strikes in that particular area are common due to the bedrock. Being in the dark without power is unpleasant and inconvenient and can be very scary for small children. No cooking, no television or computers and no moving about without seeing where you are going. It is certainly very frustrating when you are halfway through preparing the evening meal. Life becomes totally interrupted, but when the light finally whirrs back on, you are suddenly immersed in its brilliance and life begins again.

Being in the dark limits our ability to work out where things are and to function properly. On the other hand it can be a place to hide! But either way it's not a place where we were created to live out our lives.

Darkness is not a desirable state, and we were not meant to dwell there. Jesus came to dispel the darkness. Recently there was a study done to observe the effects of sensory depravation on people who were kept in solitary confinement and complete darkness for long periods of time. Torture, if you like.

Volunteers were asked to submit to forty-eight hours of isolation in total darkness. Only the observers had any visibility as they had infra-red cameras or night vision. It was observed that within twenty-four hours volunteers began to hallucinate. Without light their brains were forming their own version of the truth and reality in which to function.

Jesus called Himself the light. We know that when we 'throw light' on something, we come to see it as it really is. Where there is light there is truth.

"When Jesus spoke again to the people, he said I am the light of the world. Whoever follows me will never walk in darkness, but will have the light of life."
Jn 8:12 (NIV)

An Australian plug has three prongs on it which only become visible once it is unplugged from the power source (the power point). A lamp without a power source is of no use, and neither are we if we are not plugged into our power source as believers. An unplugged lamp sits in darkness. There are three main reasons for being unplugged and sitting in darkness.

## 1. Choice

Remaining in darkness can actually be a choice. Really, it is an act of disobedience; a refusal to acknowledge the truth that stems from either defiance or fear. In defiance we are like the people in the darkness study who hallucinated and formed their own perception of the truth. To choose to stand in the light can take courage as it means facing the truth that is then brought to light. Yet to refuse to come to the light isolates us from God's blessing and healing. In my profession as a Veterinary Surgeon, having a good light source is essential, especially during surgery. Otoscopes are used to examine ears and endoscopes for viewing inside stomachs. Without a good light source making the correct diagnosis can be difficult. The true nature of the disease will remain hidden from view.

    A choice to stay in the darkness is really a choice to hide from the truth - a choice to live in an altered state of reality.

## 2. Circumstances

Like Jeremiah we can find ourselves in a dark place due to the circumstances around us. Circumstances we have generated ourselves or that just seem to happen to us. Jeremiah was in a state of depression. God had called him to bring a message to a people who did not want to hear it and as a result Jeremiah is persecuted and ostracised.

Nothing seemed to go right for him. He was even carted off to Egypt by the Jews fleeing the Babylonians against His will. Jeremiah prophesied that they should have gone to Babylon but they were afraid and refused. Their disobedience would only bring disaster and death.

Even though Jeremiah lived in dark times, he was not isolated from God. Even though we might walk through the "Valley of the Shadow of Death", God is still with us there. Life may not always be pleasant, and such times can see a great testing of our faith and reliance on God. The danger of such times is that we allow the darkness around us to separate us from the light.

## 3. Condemnation or Correction

From Psalm 107 we see that being confined to darkness can be a form of punishment:

"Some sat in darkness and the deepest gloom, prisoners suffering
in iron chains, for they had rebelled against the words of God and
despised the counsel of the Most High. So he subjected them to
bitter labour; they stumbled, and there was no one to help.
Then they cried to the Lord in their trouble, and he saved them
from their distress. He brought them out of darkness and the
deepest gloom and broke away their chains."
Psa 107:10-14 (NIV)

Rather than being full of fire and brimstone, Hell could well be a place of total darkness – a place of eternal solitary confinement. Jesus actually says this of those who refuse His invitation to join Him in the kingdom of heaven.

"And I say to you that many will come from east and west, and sit down with Abraham, Isaac, and Jacob in the kingdom of heaven. "But the sons of the kingdom will be cast out into outer darkness. [Where] There will be weeping and gnashing of teeth."
Mat 8:11-12 (NKJV)

God may actually allow the darkness and its unpleasantness into our lives, as a consequence of our own disobedience, in the hope that we will come to our senses and return to the light, ie: cry out to him in our distress. Pain shouts out to us our need to turn back to God!

Repentance reconnects us with God.
It plugs us into the power of God.

When we have the Holy Spirit dwelling in us we cannot remain in darkness, and nor can those around us. We are lamps to the world, but unless we remain plugged into the power we are not much use to anyone. It is not just a matter of walking within the light, but walking with the light within us.

Just like Jeremiah we will not always be well received by a world that does not want to hear or see the truth. Satan prefers that we are kept in the dark when it comes to sin, that we might choose to believe that it (sin) does not exist and that perhaps God does not exist either.

When we dwell in darkness we live in isolation and fear, stumbling continually because we cannot see the reality in which we dwell, all the while denying its existence.

"This is the message we have heard from him and declare to you: God is light; in him there is no darkness at all. If we claim to have fellowship with him yet walk in the darkness, we lie and do not live by the truth. But if we walk in the light, as he is in the light, we have fellowship with one another."
1 Jn 1:5-7 (NIV)

When you're plugged into God, you've got the power!

God Moments

## Chapter Eleven:
### God moments can happen when you're
# sharing time with friends...

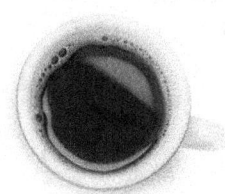

God Moments

# The Yoke of Freedom

Sometime ago I spoke with a friend who is a nurse and works as the manager of a nursing home. Having watched my father languish and eventually die in one of these places at the early age of sixty-two after twenty years of suffering, I have absolutely no desire to ever get to the stage where I myself need to become a resident of one. Yet in my discussions I came to understand that even in this final season, people can have great purpose and meaningful impact on the lives of others.

Unfortunately that is not always the case for some people as my friend recounted the story of a mother whose son had suffered brain damage after drinking kerosene at the age two. That mother carried within her the guilt of this accident for the rest of her life. As a result she suffered numerous illnesses and underwent countless surgeries.

We can all carry baggage with us through life, but it does not have to be that way. I was involved with leading children's club for awhile at a church in Sydney when my children were in primary school. We dramatised passages from "The Pilgrims Progress" during one of our teaching series. One of the most memorable scenes for me was when Pilgrim finally comes to stand at the base of the Cross. As he stares at the Cross, the large burden he has been carrying on his back loosens and rolls of him. It continues on tumbling over and over until it disappears in the mouth of a tomb that is next to the cross. Christian then leaps up for joy, his step light and his heart full of gladness as he continues on his way to the Celestial City.

Jesus says to us;

"Come to me all who are weary and burdened and I will give you rest. Take my yoke upon you and learn from me for I am gentle and humble in heart and you will find rest for your souls. For my yoke is easy and my burden is light."
Mat 11:28-30 (NIV)

You have probably seen pictures of the bullock dray carts that were the heavy duty transport vehicles of the early pioneering days of Australia. I am told that some of my forebears travelled up from Tasmania in one of them in order to settle in Queensland. The bullocks were harnessed together with wooden yokes over their shoulders. The bullockies would crack their whips over their heads, working them as a team so that they would bear on the load together. The yoke was necessary as it was intended to keep the beasts together so that they could move freely in the direction that the bullockies needed them to go.

Are you struggling to go forward burdened down by the guilt or shame of some past wrong doing? What excuses do you keep making to prevent your burden from being loosened from your back? Do you find it hard to receive or to give forgiveness? If so, such an attitude is arrogant and disobedient. Jesus died for the forgiveness of all sin. That includes your sin.

So what kind of yoke would you prefer to walk under – one of fear or one of forgiveness?

Obedience leads to freedom. By choosing to submit to the yoke of Jesus' love and forgiveness we can be assured of always finding a place of comfort at the end of our journey.

"Listen my son; accept what I say and the years of your life
will be many. I will guide you in the paths of wisdom and lead
you along straight paths. When you walk your steps will not
be hampered and when you run you will not stumble"
Prv 4:10-11 (NIV)

Sometimes we need to drop our bundle!

# The School Reunion

Recently I went to a thirty-five year high school reunion. I remember going to the twenty year union and at the time thinking how old the thirty year reunion people looked. Now I was joining their ranks! Where had all the years gone. Where indeed?

At this particular reunion there were some people who had not been back to the school since graduating. I chatted with some of them and heard them recount where life had taken them in the meantime. These were people I would never have dared speak to at school, let alone associate with.

I never really enjoyed my time at high school. In fact it would be correct to say I was dreadfully unhappy, from a social perspective anyway. It seemed to me that I was always on the outside looking in, but never fitting into the world where others seemed to bask in the sunshine of contentment, something that totally eluded me at the time. It was a hard thing for me to decide to go to the reunion because of those negative feelings that had permeated my entire school experience. Yet I felt urged to go.

In talking with some of my former colleagues, I very soon came to appreciate just what a place of blessing I am in now. One in particular spoke of his troubles and difficulties as a teenager that had wounded him physically and emotionally. Wounds, that after all these years he was still trying to come to terms with.

My eyes were opened. I had been so totally self absorbed in my own world of misery that I had failed to recognise that others had also struggled. Some had far worse situations than me to cope with. I had always felt so alone, but the reality had been vastly different.

Yet for me, I had arrived at a very different destination in life.

This was my story:

"He lifted me out of the slimy pit, out of the mud and mire; he set my feet on a rock and gave me a firm place to stand. He put a new song in my mouth, a hymn of praise to our God. Many will see and fear and put their trust in the LORD."
Psa 40:2-3 (NIV)

I now knew that this was why I had felt urged to go. God had wanted me to finally grasp the true perspective of my past life from where I stood now. This was not to make light of the pain I had suffered as a teenager, for that been very real. This was to get over it!

A pit is still a pit - whether you are standing in it or looking into it! It's the perspective that's different.

# Gift Wrapped

What do you immediately think of if someone mentions Christmas? I bet you immediately thought of... "Gifts". We all love to receive gifts. As a small child, Christmas was the most exciting time of the year. We always had a real cut pine tree which my father would procure for us. It filled the entire centre of our living room, all the way up to the ceiling and permeated the house with a pungent pine fragrance.

On Christmas Eve we would always leave out a glass of milk and biscuit for you know who and then skip gleefully to bed, snuggling under covers with dreamy expectations of what the morning might bring. On Christmas morning, there was always a psychedelic profusion of neatly wrapped gifts that encircled the base of the tree. Oh the ecstatic joy of discovering with eager fingers, the wonders concealed by the wrapping paper!

When I was about five or six years old, I remember getting a cowgirl outfit complete with a silver gun in a leather holster. Such gifts would probably be frowned upon today by the politically correct parents of this generation, but I loved that gun. It was the variety you could put cap paper into and fire at make believe Indian enemies. Hmm... I can still smell that whiff of burnt gunpowder after firing it.

While you may expect a gift from Santa this Christmas (even if Santa is your uncle dressed up in a red suit with a mobile cushion for a belly), you are probably not expecting one from God. It's common to receive gifts from a "Secret Santa" but whoever gets a gift labelled "from your Secret God"?!

Yet God does have a gift for us and it's one of those perpetual gifts, a gift that keeps on giving. (And no, I don't mean one of those gifts that you received from a well meaning relative that gets recycled at the next gift giving opportunity!)

God's gift came wrapped in the flesh of a tiny baby that would one day stretch his hands out on the beams of a rough hewn cross. These are the hands that today stretch out to us and beckon us to come to know God as a friend. I no longer have my silver gun and my cowgirl outfit wore out a long time ago, but I have God's perpetual gift - Jesus. His gift of abundant life to all who will grasp His hand of friendship.

Gift giving is always a two-way affair. While we can generally cover all bases with our gift list, there's always the unexpected gift. If you are like me, this then immediately creates an intense obligation to return the favour in kind, which usually means another trip to the shops. Pondering over the possibilities and weighing up the probabilities of my selection hitting the "acceptable" button as opposed to "gift recycling or to be allocated to the back of a cupboard" button. Oh the joys and angst of Christmas gift giving!

Have you considered that God might be expecting a gift from you this Christmas? Paul urged us in Rom 12:1 to offer ourselves to God as living sacrifices.

If you are rapt with God's gift for you, get yourself gift wrapped for God!

Not too much to ask is it? Just your whole life. After all, Jesus gave His for you!

# No Time to Say Goodbye

Recently a friend shared with me over coffee her enthusiasm about a book she was reading. It was one of those life encouragement books that gives the reader pointers on how to face the curve balls that life tends to throw at you; on how to respond to them in a positive rather than negative manner. She told me the writer encouraged readers to treat each day as if it were their last.

I know that sounds a fairly noble sentiment, but I said I didn't exactly agree with it nor did I think it was a very practical approach to life. "After all," as I said to her, "if you really were living today as your last, you probably won't be sitting here casually drinking coffee with me."

I commented, "I never get up thinking that way about the day. To do as the author suggested would make for a frenetic pace of life. I just prefer to live each day as it comes, rather than rushing around as if it were my last with so much to do; so many people to see!"

My perspective was a little different from the book's author. I already knew each day counted.

'How so!" my friend asked. I further explained that I can always wake up and take with me into each day an innate peace and contentment because I know that should I draw my last breath that day, my life has had meaning. That is because God is there every day and walks with me. I can leave this world with an assurance that I'm heading for an eternity with Him.

Not all of us know when we will draw our last breath. When my father-in-law was dying of cancer, he knew and we all knew when he was going to die. As a family we were able to gather around him together and to be with him and to say our good-byes.

My thirty-two year old brother-in-law did not know that when he left home one Saturday morning to play cricket like he had many times before, that it would be the last time he would see my sister who was six months pregnant and his two small daughters. Neither did they. It was just like any other Saturday morning. He had everything to live for, life was great. Six months previously he'd had a life changing experience and had been born again and filled with the Holy Spirit. Here was a young man who was on fire for God with a passion.

My brother-in-law did not know that as he buckled up his cricket pads and walked out onto the pitch that it would be for the last time.

As he waited for the ball to be bowled he did not know that he would never see it come, for in that moment of waiting he drew his last breath and was gone. Without warning his pacemaker had failed.

Though he did not know when he got up that morning that by the end of that day his body would be in a morgue, he knew for certain that one day he would be spending life in eternity with God no matter how the day ended.

If you are reading this and do not have that inner contentment and peace about where you will spend eternity, I urge you today to give your heart to Jesus Christ. We cannot always know when we are going to draw our last breath, but we can know with certainty where we will spend eternity. There is no need to be consciously concerned about living each day as if it were your last. Every day and every breathe counts when you walk in fellowship with Jesus Christ. He gives that inner peace that goes with you everywhere, if you place your trust in Him and His promises.

Give your life to Jesus today, So that...

"...the God of hope [will] fill you with all joy and peace ...
that you may abound in hope by the power of the Holy Spirit."
Rom 15:13 (NKJV)

...for who knows where you will be tomorrow!

You do not have an eternity to choose whom you shall follow, just an eternity dependant on the choice!

## Chapter Twelve:
### God moments can happen
# Any old how...

# Taking the Journey

I have shared with you in this book a number of thought "bytes" from my corner of life's experiences. I hope they have inspired and encouraged you and perhaps even amused you. The greatest story that we can tell anyone about God is our own story. It is the story that is most real to us and the one we are most passionate about, simply because it is about us.

Jesus didn't just preach to the multitudes, He told them stories. Just consider how many times in the Gospels that when Jesus responded to a question, instead of answering with a theological monologue, He would tell a story. It would go something like this;

"the kingdom of heaven is like a vineyard owner" (Mat 20:1) "...or a man who gave a banquet..." (Mat 22:2).

I'm sure many of the stories would have had a factual basis in the real live events of His time and if viewed through the social context of His time, many of them are probably full of an irony and humour that we don't always get with our Twenty-First Century perspective.

These stories encapsulated great spiritual truths and were readily remembered by the hearers. Even though both stories and theological sermons can transmit great truths; stories well told, will engage and entertain a listener whereas a sermon or a diatribe that labours a point will often bore. We do well to bear this in mind when we are trying to tell someone about God!

Anyone who has encountered the Living God and survived, has a "tale to tell". That includes you and me. So do not be ashamed of what you have to say or consider it insignificant. Cultivate your encounters with God because He is always there in our lives, teaching and encouraging us to grow in our understanding of just what a great blessing it is "to have a Friend in Jesus".

I hope also that through the recounting of my "God moments" you have come to see that if you're waiting around for God to audibly shout His life directions, you will be disappointed. Not only that, but you will miss out on so much of what God really is communicating to you, endlessly through the stuff of everyday living.

I have learnt over the years that by waiting around doing nothing, God will appear to be deafeningly silent. For good reason too! God calls us all to journey with Him but His directions for the journey generally only come once we have actually committed to the journey; when we, ourselves, on our own, have made a decision to move and step out according to the prompting of our hearts desires and passions often originally placed there by God. Be assured, guidance will come along the way if you are actively seeking it and not just passively waiting for God to somehow just drop it on you.

I have met many who were not willing to start the journey; to even take just a few faltering steps, just because they are afraid. Should I or shouldn't I do this or that. Continually vacillating and never making any active decision to move in any direction. Always fearful: Fearful of failing, fearful of not having heard correctly from God before starting; fearful of not knowing where the journey will end.

Fear is the most powerful mind manipulating tool in the Enemy's armoury. You will have noticed that many of my stories have focused on facing our fears. Fear paralyses our faith and neutralises our trust in God.

There is nothing wrong in acknowledging before God that we have fears. That actually opens up a dialogue with God. Looking at our weaknesses full in the face is the starting place of our strength. To refuse to start the journey is to stand before God in disobedience and rebellion. Consider what happened to the servant in Matthew Chapter 25 who, out of fear, buried his one talent. The dark place of teeth gnashing and weeping was his reward! This is the end place of all who make fear their friend.

There have definitely been times in my life when I felt that I was losing my way and that there really was no light at the end of the tunnel. It was in these dark times that I have been greatly encouraged by these verses in Psalms:

> "If the LORD delights in a man's way, he makes his steps firm;
> though he stumble, he will not fall, for the LORD upholds him
> with his hand."
> Psa 37:23-24 (NIV)

You see it doesn't matter if we get it wrong sometimes and stumble. It matters that we are intent on journeying with God; that the desire of our heart is to mesh our will with His. When we do wander off, get sided tracked and confused, God is there. He is always there, closer than our next breath, ready to prune, refine and re-refocus us, so that we can continue to go forward with Him in the right direction.

Consider the wise men that came to see Jesus as a baby. They set out on a journey to find a king whose birth was foretold in ancient prophesies. They were not told beforehand exactly where they would find him or even how long it might take. But guidance came along the way, in the form of a star. It would not have been an easy journey and certainly they would have been venturing into places that none of them had ever been before and more than likely would have encountered many unforeseen dangers along the way. If they had waited for undeniable confirmation before leaving that their journey would be 100 percent safe and successful, they might never have left.

Theirs was a journey of faith. A faith journey that to their surprise brought them not just to a king but into a worshipping relationship with the Creator of the star they had been following.

So it is with us. Our entire life walk with God is a faith journey. It is a journey God wants us all to take. Do we always know where we are going? ...No. Will it always be safe? ...No. Will you always be happy and pain free?...No.

However, it will be the adventure of a lifetime. The purpose and end point of which is the same regardless of who you are and what dreams you might have. It is to bring us all into an eternal worshiping relationship with the Living God, our Creator, our King and our Friend.

The journey itself is just as important as reaching the journey's end.

In fact you might say that the journey is actually the goal, for it is along the way, through the stuff of life, that God reveals Himself to us.

My prayer is that once you put this book down, you too will be up for the adventure of a lifetime with God!

## Balthazar

The dewy air rose with us in stirrup leathers
as dawning rays caressed our chilly cheeks
with a subtle warmth, beckoning cheerfully to the day.
The morning of our beginning, to traverse
unrequited dreams of prophets long since perished.

But now the wind it scratches at our faces with its horey
nails of grit.
Oh to be reposed upon cushioned comfort
and bathed in cinnamon breeze
where tasselled serving girls proffer honey cakes
and iced teas infused with bergamot.
Not here swathed in sweltered heat astride a dromedary.

Can a path be found within a celestial pool
with glimmering shapes that ripple
and swirl across an ebony sky?
Where Jupiter and Saturn join and royalty proclaim
will there a king be found?
Gasper says, It is so! So onward we must go.

Our gift swelled saddle bags effused with scent
of frankincense and myrrh concealed therein,
when arrayed in splendour at regal feet
will mark our journeys end. But now I fear
Will all end in plunder, just a bandits delight?
Melchior says, Hold back the fright, stick fast to faith.
Just keep the God child's star in sight.

Where the hawthorn meets the sycamore
Not at some great ornate palatial marble stair.
Who would have thought our journey
would have ended there?
In David's town, blood red berries adorn his royal crown.
At birth entombed within His crudely hewn dogwood throne,
Tiny hands stretch forth to greet the day banishing the night of
Wrenching travail, a mothers joy transformed
from sweated tears and groans.

Will you make the journey there?
Come away from your world of care?
Take flight from sensuous delights that tantalize and tease.
How can you know what worth is wealth
until all is left behind?
The God child's star it summons all,
not just those of wise and noble birth.
Come, your journeying with danger will be fraught,
that is true,
But in its ending you will find your beginning.
The Way is clear, it's Light will guide
and make each footfall sure
Tiny hands they call. Come with me then and on bended knee
Our gifts we'll lay before a crudely hewn blood stained
dogwood throne.

Kate Case - 2011

God Moments

www.ingramcontent.com/pod-product-compliance
Lightning Source LLC
Chambersburg PA
CBHW052027290426
44112CB00014B/2412